I0816978

Viella History, Art and Humanities Collection
13

Julian Gardner

Fracta Doces

Thirteenth-Century Insular Visitors to Rome

viella

Copyright © 2022 - Viella s.r.l.
All rights reserved
First edition: September 2022
ISBN 979-12-5469-018-5

GARDNER, Julian
Fracta doces : thirteenth-century insular visitors to Rome / Julian Gardner. - Roma : Viella, 2022. - 109 p., [14] c. di tav. : ill. ; 24 cm. - (Viella history, art and humanities collection ; 13)
Bibliografia: p. [87]-103
Indice dei nomi: p. [105]-109
ISBN 979-12-5469-018-5
1. Roma - Descrizioni [di] Viaggiatori inglesi - Sec. 13.
914.563204 (DDC 23.ed) Scheda bibliografica: Biblioteca Fondazione Bruno Kessler

viella
libreria editrice
via delle Alpi, 32
I-00198 ROMA
tel. 06 84 17 758
fax 06 85 35 39 60
www.viella.it

Contents

Acknowledgements

The origins of this monograph lie in a paper delivered at a conference in Naples organised by Bianca De Divitiis. Earlier versions were tried out on audiences at Oxford and the Warburg Institute. I have had much help from friends, Mary Carruthers, Angela Dressen, Ingo Herklotz, Dale Kinney, Charles Little, John Osborne, Valentino Pace and Serena Romano. Dott.ssa Manuela Gianandrea and Professor Manfred Luchterhand generously provided me with copies of their work, then inaccessible in Britain *in tempore pestilentiae*. The resources of the Bodleian Library have been fundamental to the enterprise. My main debt is to my wife Christa Gardner von Teuffel, for her unfailing encouragement and support.

Eine Welt zwar bist du, o Rom; doch ohne die Liebe
Wäre die Welt nicht die Welt, wäre denn Rom auch nicht Rom.

Goethe, *Römische Elegien*

Preface

Adam of Usk was a passionate Welshman. He had risen through his own abilities, of which he thought highly, and had played, he claimed, a central part in the lethal student riots at the University of Oxford in 1388-1389 as leader of the Welsh faction. He went to Rome primarily in search of preferment, and his *Chronicle* provides an unusual external light on a troubled period in Rome's history.[1] Adam soon achieved a prestigious post as auditor in the apostolic palace, and aspired to an English bishopric. He was nominated first to the see at Hereford, the nearest diocese to his hometown, and subsequently to that at St David's, the same Welsh archbishopric on which the ambitions of his earlier compatriot Gerald of Wales had foundered some two centuries before. Like Gerald, Adam was stymied by his nationality: the English establishment could not trust a Welshman.

Adam's Roman interlude lasted from 1402 until 1406. The metropolis was, if anything, more dilapidated than it had been at the time of Gerald's visits. He found the city repellent and its inhabitants disgusting. His *Chronicle* recorded a common night-time occupation:

> I had lodgings close to St. Peter's palace, I often used to get up in the night to observe the behaviour of the wolves and the dogs. Although the watchdogs used to bark at the doors of their masters' houses to protect them, the wolves would carry off the smaller dogs virtually under the noses of the bigger ones, and despite the fact that the little ones howled even more loudly as they were being dragged away, in the hope of being rescued by the bigger ones, these big ones would do nothing about it except to bark even more; it seemed to me not dissimilar to the sort of comradeship shown by the powers that be to those who have been cast out from their country to wander through the forests.[2]

During the anti-papal riots at Rome in 1405, Adam was forced to disguise himself as a Dominican friar and to go into hiding to avoid being lynched. He left more rapidly than Gerald and even more furtively than Thomas of Marlborough, another insular visitor who will appear in the following pages.

Rome was a moving target. Notoriously, it was where the pope resided. Thus, when the "new" Rome was established at Avignon, many ambitious clerics from

1. Christopher Given-Wilson, *The Chronicle of Adam Usk 1377-1421*, Oxford, Oxford University Press, 1997.
2. Given-Wilson, *The Chronicle*, p. 194.

Britain found it more enticing. It was easier to reach, and the climate and the wine were superior. About 1319, Stephen of Kettelbergh wrote to his friend John Lutterell, former chancellor of the University of Oxford, alerting him to the possibilities on the banks of the Rhône.[3] The new pope, a lawyer by training, had realised that the law was inadequate to treat the foundations of ecclesiastical power and now saw the need for theologians; if one were to cobble together a couple of attractive disputations, the place would be a gold mine.[4] A bishopric, even an archbishopric, could be the prize. At Avignon, Lutterell participated in the commission of enquiry into the writings of William Ockham, and reaped valuable livings.[5]

Gerald, like Adam and Lutterell, sought advancement. He preceded Adam in the autobiographical content of his writings – often seeing the vicissitudes of his own career as a metaphor of his times. Of the four remarkable visitors who visited Rome in the period circumscribed by the pontificates of Innocent III (1198-1216), Honorius III (1216-1227) and Gregory IX (1227-1241), he was probably the most learned and certainly the vainest. Gervase of Tilbury, like Gerald a member of the ruling Anglo-Norman elite, was essentially a *flâneur* in the service of a ne'er-do-well emperor. Master Gregory, the most mysterious and the most penetrating of the insular visitors, is our primary guide for the antiquities of Rome, which he personally inspected. The churches were a distraction, useful markers for the location of antiquities. Thomas of Marlborough was a monastic litigant who, to an extent that flabbergasted even himself, won his court case in the Roman Curia and became Abbot of Evesham largely on the back of that success. We know little more of his background than we do that of Gregory.

These men shared a common educational background, but little else. Gerald was a scion of the Anglo-Norman aristocracy that had established itself in Wales, while Gervase was a courtier. Thomas, like Gerald, was a student at Paris University, and disputes with the Bishop of Worcester over the status of his abbey at Evesham propelled him to Rome. Although Master Gregory's career is shrouded in mystery, he was demonstrably well-connected and also highly educated. All could cite the classics by heart; all were fascinated by their experiences and wrote down what they saw, and often what they thought. It is these men whose experiences of Rome we shall examine in the following pages.

3. Herbert E. Salter, ed., *Snappe's Formulary and Other Records*, Oxford, Oxford University Press, 1924, pp. 304-305; Jean Dunbabin, "Careers and Vocations", in *The History of the University of Oxford*, vol. I, ed. by Jeremy I. Catto, Oxford, Oxford University Press, 1984, pp. 565-605: 580.

4. Sylvain Piron, "Avignon sous Jean XXII, l'Eldorado des théologiens", in *Jean XXII et le Midi (Cahiers de Fanjeaux 45)*, ed. by Michelle Fournié and Daniel le Blévec, Toulouse, Privat, 2012, pp. 358-391; William J. Courtenay, "The Academic and Intellectual Worlds of Ockham", in *The Cambridge Companion to Ockham*, ed. by Paul Vincent Spade, Cambridge, Cambridge University Press, 1999, pp. 17-30: 25.

5. William J. Courtenay, "Theology and Theologians from Ockham to Wyclif", in *The History of the University of Oxford*, vol. II, ed. by Jeremy I. Catto and Ralph Evans, Oxford, Oxford University Press, 1992, pp. 1-34: 16-17.

1. *Dramatis personae*

The personalities and social contexts of two early 13th-century Anglo-Norman observers of the Roman landscape, Gerald of Wales (Giraldus Cambrensis) and Gervase of Tilbury, are relatively well-known. A third, Magister Gregorius, or Master Gregory, whose report on the monuments of Rome in the 13th century is uniquely important, is only dimly known as a personality and difficult to place either in time or place of origin. A fourth, who may serve as a kind of control, Thomas of Marlborough, was proctor and later abbot of the exempt Benedictine Abbey of Evesham in Worcestershire and also spent a significant period at the curia. However, his mind was typically on more mundane things, like winning his case and evading his creditors.[1] Thomas, like Gerald, was inclined to view the contemporary world through his own prism.

Some time after 1208, Gerald composed what amounts to an incomplete autobiography, the *De rebus a se gestis* (*The Events of His Own Life*).[2] This can be complemented by passages from his later *De iure et statu Menevenensis Ecclesiae* (*On the Rights and Status of the Church of St David's*), which was composed between 1215 and 1218, shortly before the date he is presumed to have died. We can also draw on the slightly earlier *De invectionibus* (*On Shameful Attacks*); both texts are concerned with the dispute about the bishopric of St David's in West Wales. From this, we can deduce that Gerald's life was dominated by two preoccupations: himself, and his ultimately unsuccessful struggle to succeed his uncle as bishop of St David's. Other autobiographical details are scattered throughout his voluminous writings, which occupy eight substantial volumes in the Rolls Series.

1. Thomas of Marlborough, *History of the Abbey of Evesham*, ed. by Jane E. Sayers and Leslie Watkiss, Oxford, Oxford University Press, 2003, pp. 344-346; Jane E. Sayers, "English Benedictine Monks at the Papal Court in the Thirteenth Century: The Experience of Thomas of Marlborough in a Wider Context", *Journal of Medieval Monastic Studies*, 2 (2013), pp. 109-129. Similarities in the cases had already been noted in M. Spaethen, "Giraldus Cambrensis und Thomas von Evesham über die von ihnen an der Kurie geführten Prozesse", *Neues Archiv*, 31 (1906), pp. 595-649.

2. A detailed chronology of Gerald's writings forms an appendix to Robert Bartlett, *Gerald of Wales: A Voice of the Middle Ages*, Stroud, History Press, reprint 2013, appendix, pp. 174-180. Gerald continually revised his works, and many of them exist in different recensions.

One thing we learn about Gerald is his personal appearance. He was incorrigibly vain and regarded himself as strikingly attractive. While visiting Archbishop Baldwin of Forde at Blockley in Worcestershire in the early 1180s, he noted complacently: "I was a young man at the time, with nature's bounty of delicate features – they were not to last – and greatly distinguished by my handsome physique",[3] and "the Cistercian abbot Serlo, who was also present at the meeting, immediately remarked on my good looks".[4] Towards the end of his life, while writing the *De iure et statu Menevensis Ecclesiae*, vol. V, he returned to the subject of his personal appearance, noting his particularly bushy eyebrows.[5] This pervasive vanity means that he was the only visitor to medieval Rome of whom I am aware who spoke so extensively about his personal appearance in his writings. Gerald clearly regarded himself more as a protagonist than a simple reporter, but also as a liminal figure who was striving to be heard.[6]

We can deduce a good deal about Gervase, who is personally much more reticent, from the *Otia Imperialia* (*Recreations for an Emperor*), the elaborate literary *divertissement* he presented to Holy Roman Emperor Otto IV in 1214 or 1215.[7] Gervase was from Tilbury in Essex and was related to Patrick, first Earl of Salisbury. Like Gerald, then, he was a member of the Anglo-Norman elite. He was also a few years younger, having been born in the late 1150s or early in the next decade. Like Gerald, he had also enjoyed an excellent education, studying and then teaching canon law at the University of Bologna. A pupil of his, Giovanni Pignatelli, whom he visited in 1190, had become Archdeacon of Naples. His bureaucratic career easily eclipsed that of his Welsh contemporary. He was a

3. *Giraldi Cambrensis Opera*, 8 vols, ed. by John S. Brewer, James F. Dimock and George F. Warner, London, Longman and Co., 1861-1891 [hereafter *GC Opera*]. For this quotation, see vol. IV, *Speculum ecclesiae*, ed. by John S. Brewer, London, Longman and Co., 1873, p. 104: "Eram autem tunc adolescens, statura procerus, facie quoque fragilique ac momentaneo naturae bono, formae nitore praeclarus…"; Gerald of Wales, *The Journey Through Wales and Description of Wales*, ed. and transl. by Lewis Thorpe, Harmondsworth, Penguin Books, 1978, p. 23.

4. *GC Opera*, vol. IV, p. 104: "Putasne ullatenus mori possit 'tam pulchra iuventus'?"; Maurice Powicke, "Gerald of Wales", *Bulletin of the John Rylands Library*, 12 (1928), pp. 389-410: 396, reprinted in Maurice Powicke, *The Christian Life in the Middle Ages*, Oxford, Oxford University Press, 1935, pp. 107-129: 115. The quotation is from Ovid, *Metamorphoses*, VII, 514. Powicke rightly remarks that "Gerald lived every day an existence of dramatic egotism".

5. *GC Opera*, vol. III, *De invectionibus, de jure et statu Menevensi ecclesiae*, ed. by John S. Brewer, London, Longman, Green, Longman and Roberts, 1983, p. 293: "…per descriptionem sibi factam, tam staturae grandis quam superciliorum quoque grandium et hirsutorum, ipsum recognovit, maxime vero per supercilia".

6. John F. Benton, "Consciousness of Self and Perceptions of Individuality", in *Renaissance and Renewal in the Twelfth Century*, ed. by Robert L. Benson and Giles Constable, Oxford, Oxford University Press, 1982, pp. 263-295: 266.

7. Gervase of Tilbury, *Otia Imperialia: Recreation for an Emperor*, ed. by Shelagh Banks and James Binns, Oxford, Oxford University Press, 2002; Shelagh Banks, "Tilbury, Gervase of", in *Dictionary of National Biography*, vol. LIV, Oxford, Oxford University Press, 2004, pp. 774-775; Henry G. Richardson, "Gervase of Tilbury", *History*, 46 (1961), pp. 102-114. Antonia Gransden, *Historical Writing in England*, 2 vols, vol. I, c. 550 to c. 1307, London, Routledge, 1994, p. 324 regards him as a *littérateur*.

familiar of Guillaume de Blois, archbishop of Reims (1176-1202). Then, by the 1180s, he was in the service of William II of Sicily, who presented him with a house at Nola, some thirty kilometres east of Naples. He is also documented at Arles in 1201 in the service of Archbishop Imbert d'Aiguières (1198-1202).

Soon after, he joined the court of Emperor Otto IV and may have accompanied him to Rome for the imperial coronation in October 1209, although his first certain link with Otto is at Tarascon in 1214. Later, in 1221, Gervase is documented at Arles, where Otto was to retire after his calamitous defeat at the Battle of Bouvines (27 July 1214). As an imperial official at Arles, Gervase was involved in an arbitration over Les Alyscamps, the largest open-air collection of ancient sarcophagi that was accessible during the Middle Ages.[8] Arles also possessed very notable Roman ruins, and its impressive amphitheatre must have made Gervase recall his Roman experience. He was evidently a polished courtier with an anecdote ready for every occasion.

Scholars still debate the identity and chronology of Master Gregory, whose treatise on the marvels of Rome, the *Narracio de mirabilibus Urbis Romae*, survives in an unique manuscript now preserved at St Catherine's College, Cambridge.[9] It seems highly likely that Gregory served as chancellor to Ottone da Tonengo and was sent to England as cardinal legate by Pope Gregory IX in 1237-1240.[10] An entry in the Patent Rolls for May 1238 lists Gregory as receiving an

8. Joseph-Hyacinthe Albanès, *Gallia Christiana Novissima Histoire des Archevêchés, Évêchés et Abbayes de France, Arles*, 7 vols, Valence, Imprimerie Valentinoise, 1901, no. 873, col. 343, 4 June 1221: judgement for Eldiardis abbess S. Césaire "...super absolutione cimiterii de Aliscampis [...] cum libera sepultura illorum qui ibi sepeliebantur". See no. 2628, dated 13 June 1221. The arbitrators were "Raimundus prepositi Arelaten et magistri Gervasii in regno Arelaten imperialis aule marescalli". Eugène Duprat, "Histoire des Légendes Saintes de Provence", *Mémoires de l'Institut Historique de Provence*, 17 (1940), pp. 118-198; 18 (1941), pp. 87-186: 108 prints the full text of the 11 June 1221 arbitration on pp. 153-157. See also Falko Neininger, *Konrad von Urach († 1227) Zähringer, Zisterzienser, Kardinallegat*, Paderborn, Schöningh, 1994. The dispute over Les Alyscamps with Gervase of Tilbury is discussed on p. 268 and in Pietro Pressutti, *Regesta Honorii Papae III iussu et munificentia Leonis XIII pontificis maximi ex Vaticanis archetypis aliisque fontibus edidit*, Rome, Typographia Vaticana, 1888-1895, no. 85, p. 333; no. 123, p. 356, 15 June 1222 (Albanès no. 873 gives an incorrect date). See Neininger, *Konrad von Urach*, no. 21, pp. 541-551 for the full text of the document.

9. MS 3 (formerly E 4 96); *Magister Gregorius (XIIe ou XIIIe siècle), Narracio de Mirabilibus Romae*, ed. by Robert H. C. Huygens, Leiden, Brill, 1970; *Master Gregorius: The Marvels of Rome*, ed. and transl. by John Osborne, Toronto, Pontifical Institute of Medieval Studies, 1987. See also Cristina Nardella, *Il fascino di Roma nel medioevo. Le "meraviglie di Roma" di maestro Gregorio*, Rome, Viella, 1997; Gordon Rushforth, "Magister Gregorius de Mirabilibus Urbis Romae: A New Description of Rome in the Twelfth Century", *Journal of Roman Studies*, 9 (1919), pp. 14-58. The manuscript in Cambridge is reproduced in colour in *Wunder Roms im Blick des Nordens von der Antike bis zur Gegenwart*, ed. by Cristoph Stiegemann, Petersberg, Michael Imhof, 2017, cat. entry no. 51, pp. 358-360 (colour illustrations of fol. 190r and fols 201v-202r). The entry by the College Librarian Colin Higgins is uninformative and dated.

10. Josiah C. Russell, *Dictionary of Writers of Thirteenth Century England*, London, Longmans Green, 1936, pp. 40-41; Agostino Paravicini-Bagliani, *Cardinali di Curia e "Familiae" Cardinalizie dal 1227 al 1254*, 2 vols, vol. I, Padua, Antenore, 1972, p. 94. Pietro

annual pension of 17 marks drawn from the vacant see of Norwich. Another entry in the Liberate Rolls, which has largely gone unnoticed, suggests that he likely held a post earlier in the *familia* of Thomas de Blundeville, bishop of Norwich between 1226-1236.[11] A *contrabreve* instructed the guardian of the bishopric of Norwich "to cause Master Gregory, the legate's chancellor to have 17 marks yearly that he was wont to receive of the grant of Thomas, late bishop of Norwich, in the same way he received it in the bishop's time [...] so long as it shall be in the guardian's custody by the king's order".[12] Finally, it remains unclear whether the title of *magister*, which appears in his prologue, indicates that he was a university graduate, and, if so, from what university.[13]

Frustratingly, the only surviving manuscript of the *Narracio* omits a word, which almost certainly identified the place to which Gregory wrote of returning: "[when] I return to [missing] from this journey, I shall take the time to investigate more diligently (*exercitatiori indagatione perscrutabor*) those things which at the moment are unclear or obscure, and shall gladly share this research with my friends".[14] An episcopal *familia* could provide just such an intellectual *côterie*, but our knowledge of the early library resources of Norwich cathedral priory has been irremediably damaged by the fire of 1272. Important for our investigation, this identification suggests that the probable date for the *Narracio*'s composition was between 1226 and 1236.[15] He was thus the latest of our visitors to Rome.

Gerald, who was born in 1145 or 1146, was the youngest of the four sons of William de Barri. On his mother Angharad's side, he was related to Rhys ap Tewdwr, prince of Dyved.[16] On his father's side, Gerald was unequivocally a member of the Marcher aristocracy. This distinguished ancestry, both Welsh and Anglo-Norman, in fact made him unelectable to the episcopate in Wales, as successive English kings feared a possibly divided loyalty.[17] From infancy he seems to have been intended for the church. His childhood unfolded at the castle of Manorbier on the Pembrokeshire coast, which was "visible from afar because of its turrets and crenellations on the top of a hill, which is quite near the sea" (Fig. 1).[18]

Silanos and Ottone da Tonengo, *Dizionario Biografico degli Italiani*, vol. LXXX, Rome, Istituto della Enciclopedia italiana, 2014, pp. 4-7.

11. *Master Gregorius*, ed. by Osborne, pp. 14-15.

12. *Calendar of the Liberate Rolls Henry III*, vol. I, *A.D. 1226-1240*, London, Longmans, Green, Reader and Dyer, 1916, pp. 307-308 (7 January 1238, Westminster).

13. Nardella, *Il fascino*, p. 29.

14. Ch. 27: "Cum ex favente deo in ***** ex hac peregrinacione rediero", *ibid.*, p. 166. It is worth noting that Gregory terms his visit to Rome a pilgrimage.

15. *Master Gregorius*, ed. by Osborne, p. 15. Ranulph Higden, who uses Gregory in his very popular *Polychronicon*, was a monk of St Werburgh in Chester and never seems to have travelled much beyond Cheshire. See John Taylor, *The "Universal Chronicle" of Ranulph Higden*, Oxford, Oxford University Press, 1966, p. 1.

16. Bartlett, *Gerald of Wales: A Voice of the Middle Ages*, pp. 20-25. The most penetrating character assessment of Gerald still remains Powicke, "Gerald of Wales".

17. He complains of anti-Welsh prejudice in *GC Opera*, vol. VIII, *De principis instructione liber*, ed. by George F. Warner, London, Her Majesty's Stationery Office, 1891, p. lviii.

18. "...castellum, quod Maynaurpir dicitur [...] Stat enim hoc castrum, turribus et propugnaculis eximium in collis cujusdam capite versus murinum ab occidente portum extent";

Manorbier was "in all the broad lands of Wales [...] the most pleasant place by far", he was later to write.[19] When he played on the beach as a child, whilst his elder brothers built castles or fortifications in the sand, Gerald constructed churches or monasteries, and his doting father called him "my bishop", a status he would never attain, despite his persistent efforts.[20]

Gerald received the best education available to a boy of aristocratic status.[21] First, he studied under Master Haimo at the great Benedictine abbey of St Peter's in Gloucester, and subsequently at the University of Paris, where, to take his own estimate at face value, through dedicated study, he became extremely successful both as a student and teacher.[22] He mentions that he was a young man at the university when future French king Philip Augustus was born (August 1165). About 1175, at the relatively young age of 29, he became Archdeacon of Brecon, the apex of his ecclesiastical career, though he was not yet aware it would be so. It seems he had a competent command of Welsh and on occasion acted as interpreter for Baldwin of Forde, Archbishop of Canterbury (1185-1191).[23] Gerald had become a royal clerk at the court of Henry II, but withdrew from court life with some relief around 1196, a bitterly disappointed man.[24] He seems then to have undertaken further study at Lincoln, perhaps with William de Montibus.[25]

Gerald's maternal uncle, David Fitzgerald, had been bishop of Saint David's (1148-1176), the senior Welsh bishopric, and there was considerable expectation that the brilliant young Archdeacon would succeed him in due time. In fact, the dispute over the Welsh bishopric shaped Gerald's life. It entailed three visits to Rome (and a fourth he completed as a simple pilgrim in 1206). The longest of these visits lasted four years and afforded the inquisitive Archdeacon ample opportunity to observe the great churches of Rome and to record information not

GC Opera, vol. VI, *Itinerarium Kambriae, Descriptio Kambriae*, ed. by James F. Dimock, London, Longmans, Green, Reader and Dyer, 1868, bk I, ch. 12, p. 92; Gerald of Wales, *The Journey Through Wales and Description of Wales*, p. 150.

19. *GC Opera*, vol. VI, bk I, ch. 12: "...ut Kambriae totius locus sit hic amoenissimus"; Gerald of Wales, *The Journey Through Wales and Description of Wales*, p. 151.

20. *GC Opera*, vol. I, *De rebus a se gestis*, ed. by John S. Brewer, London, Longman, Green, Longman and Roberts, 1861, ch. 1, pp. 21-22. While his three brothers "...nunc castrum nunc oppida nunc palatia puerilibus ut solet haec aetas praeludiis in sabulo vel pulves protrahentibus, modulo suo, solus hic simili praeludio semper ecclesias eligere et monasterii construere tota intentione satagebat...", Gerald's father "...ludendo et applaudendo suum episcopum vocavit". For the castle, which preserves considerable remnants of a late 12th-century hall, see John Kenyon, "Manorbier Castle", *The Archaeological Journal*, 167 (2010), pp. 43-45; Thomas Lloyd, Julian Orbach, Robert Scourfield, *Pembrokeshire (The Buildings of Wales)*, New Haven, Yale University Press, 2004, pp. 272-274.

21. Bartlett, *Gerald of Wales: A Voice of the Middle Ages*, p. 46.

22. *GC Opera*, vol. VIII, bk 3, ch. 25, pp. 292-293: "Liberalibus animi studiis vehementer applicaret".

23. See, however, Powicke, "Gerald of Wales", p. 117; *The Journey Through Wales and Description of Wales*, ed. by Thorpe, p. 29.

24. "Curia curarum genetrix; et schola deliciarum": *GC Opera*, vol. VIII, p. lvii.

25. John W. Baldwin, *Masters, Princes and Merchants: The Social View of Peter the Chanter and His Circle*, Princeton, Princeton University Press, 1970, 2/1, p. 42.

readily available elsewhere.[26] It has also become clear that Gerald was a reformer at heart, who tried, unavailingly, to influence the central debate on church finances at the Fourth Lateran Council of 1215.

At the University of Paris, he had thoroughly absorbed the reformist ideals of Peter the Chanter.[27] Gerald was an unsparing critic of the shocking ignorance of the clergy. He was also a supporter of the radical solution delineated by Emperor Henry VI, which held that each church was to allocate a living to finance the curia and that each cathedral was to assign a tithe of its annual revenues.[28] This idea was taken up by Innocent III on his own initiative at the Fourth Lateran Council of 1215, but the pope withdrew his proposal in the face of concerted opposition. In the *Speculum ecclesiae*, which Gerald composed before the Council to publicise the need for radical financial reform, he advocated a similar step.[29] He presented an early version of the text to Stephen Langton before the Cardinal set out for the Council.[30] Once again, Gerald was to be disappointed.

The papal curia was also where the Evesham drama played out. Appeals to Rome required a personal presence at the curia.[31] As will become clear, "Rome" was a mobile concept. For Gerald, as for both Gervase and Thomas, Rome was wherever the curia was currently established. "*Ubi papa ibi Roma*" was a well-worn phrase.[32] In 1206, when Gerald made his final farewells to Innocent III, the meeting took place at Ferentino, some 65 kilometres south-east of Rome. In the first half of the 13th century, when the political situation permitted, the papacy spent most summers in the Roman Campagna, to avoid the torrid heat of the city.[33] As the papal household moved to the small satellite towns, it looked like

26. This visit was punctuated by two return visits to Britain.

27. Powicke, "Gerald of Wales", p. 125; Bartlett, *Gerald of Wales: A Voice of the Middle Ages*, pp. 14, 32, 202, n. 13; Baldwin, *Masters, Princes and Merchants*; Jessalyn Bird, *Heresy, Crusade and Reform in the Circle of Peter the Chanter*, Ph.D. Dissertation, Oxford University, 2001.

28. *GC Opera*, vol. IV, pp. 301-305; Richard Kay, "Gerald of Wales and the Fourth Lateran Council", *Viator*, 29 (1988), pp. 79-93. The Roman church, in origin amply endowed by Constantine, was now impoverished: pp. 83, 87.

29. *GC Opera*, vol. IV, pp. 301-305. H. Wyn Evans, "The Bishops of St. Davids from Bernard to Bec", in *Medieval Pembrokeshire*, ed. by R. F. Walker, Haverfordwest, Pembrokeshire Historical Society, 2002, pp. 279-311: 278-280.

30. Kay, "Gerald of Wales", p. 84; Suzanne La Vere, "'A Priest is Not a Free Person': Clerical Sins and Upholding Higher Moral Standards in the *Gemma Ecclesiastica*", in *Gerald of Wales: New Perspectives on a Medieval Writer and Critic*, ed. by Georgia Henley and Joseph Mullen, Cardiff, University of Wales Press, 2018, pp. 183-202: 197.

31. Barbara Bombi, "Petitioning between England and Avignon in the First Half of the Fourteenth Century", in *Medieval Petitions: Grace and Grievance*, ed. by W. Mark Ormerod, Gwilym Dodd and Anthony Musson, Woodbridge, York Medieval Press, 2009, pp. 64-81: 65.

32. Michele Maccarrone, "Ubi est papa, ibi est Roma", in *Aus Kirche und Reich. Studien zu Theologie, Politik und Recht im Mittelalter. Festschrift für Friedrich Kempf zu seinem fünfundsiebzigsten Geburstag und fünfzigjährigen Doktorjubiläum*, ed. by Hubert Mordek, Sigmaringen, J. Thorbecke, 1983, pp. 371-382, reprinted in *Romana Ecclesia, Cathedra Petri*, 2 vols, vol. II, ed. by Piero Zerbi, Raffaello Volpini and Alessandro Galuzzi, Rome, Herder, 1991, pp. 1137-1156.

33. Agostino Paravicini Bagliani, "La mobilità della Curia Romana nel secolo XIII. Riflessi locali", in *Società e istituzioni dell'Italia comunale: l'esempio di Perugia (secoli XII-XIV),*

an army on the march, with tents, field-kitchens and all. It produced a temporary but acute increase in the local population in the rural settings, but it was generally welcomed by the host towns, even where the papacy set conditions for its arrival.

We can glimpse how a papal summer sojourn impacted the small towns in a passage in the *Chronicle* of William, abbot of the small Benedictine house of Andres, in the diocese of Poitiers, who joined Innocent III at Viterbo in 1207/1208. He observed:

> And so never – or hardly ever – pausing, but always moving on each day when it was hardly daybreak, I came to Viterbo and there I found Rome. For, the lord pope Innocent III had left Rome for the time being because the summertime was so harmful to his body, and he stayed there as if in his own city. Both for the repose of the clerics and the laity following the court and for the infinite multitude of pilgrims arriving every day, the discreet pastor chose a wealthy city, rich in bread and wine, supplied with fodder, grass, barley, and also with health-bringing baths, surrounded by vines, woods and copses in support of those following him, and he resided there. We have indeed heard from many staying there that 40,000 men, not counting people of the city, took lodging there for a whole month together at the same time and that they, with the lord bishop Nivelo of Soissons and other noble men who were flowing in every day, were getting ready to return to Constantinople, which he had recently acquired, and nevertheless with reference to everything necessary for the human body or for horses for sale, nothing was ever the more expensive.[34]

William's report of an acutely over-crowded town, scarce lodgings and exploitative prices, combined with difficult access to the curia, demonstrates how

Perugia 6-9 novembre 1985, Perugia, 1988 pp. 155-278 remains basic. An updated version is printed in *Itineranza pontificia: mobilità della curia papale nel Lazio (secoli XII-XIII)*, ed. by Sandro Carocci, Rome, Istituto storico italiano per il medioevo, 2003, pp. 3-78. See also Sandro Carocci, "Mobilità papale e territorio: problemi di metodo e di interpretazione", in *Itineranza pontificia*, pp. 81-100.

34. *Willelmi Chronica Andrensis*, in *Monumentae Germaniae Historica, Scriptores*, vol. XXIV, ed. by Johann Heller, Hanover, Hahnsche Buchhandlung, 1879, 708, ch. 57 (reprint Stuttgart, Anton Hiersemann, 1964, pp. 684-773: 737) (1207): "Vix igitur aut nunquam moram faciens, sed omni fere die cepto itinere proficiscens, Viterbium tandem deveni et ibidem Romam inveni. Num dominus Innocentius papa tertius, propter estivum tempus corpori suo contrarium Roma ad tempus relicta tamquam in civitate propria ibi manebat, et tam propter quietem clericorum et laicocorum curiam suam sequentium quam propter infinitam multitudinem peregrinorum omni die adventantium urbem opulentam , pane et vino copiosam, feno, gramine, hordeo refertam, salubribus etiam balneis, vineis, silvis et virgultis redimitam, in subsidium se sequentium pastor discretus elegerat et ibi residebat. Audivimus enim a multis ibidem perhendinantibus, 40 milia hominum, excepto civitatis populo, per mensem integrum simul et semel mansionem fecisset cum domino Nivelone Suessoniensi episcopo et aliis viris nobilibus omni die confluentibus apud Constantinopolim, quam nuper acquisierat, regredi paratos existere, et tamen de omni venali humano corpori aut equis necessario nichil unquam carius venditum fuisse". See also William of Andres, *The Chronicle of Andres*, ed. and transl. by Leah Shopkow, Washington, Catholic University Press, 2017, pp. 186-187; Sara Menzinger, "Viterbo, 'Città papale': motivazioni e conseguenze della presenza pontificia a Viterbo nel XIII secolo", in *Itineranza pontificia*, pp. 307-340; Brenda Bolton, "A New Rome in a Small Place? Imitation and Re-Creation in the Patrimony of St Peter", in *Rome across Time and Space: Cultural Transmission and the Exchange of Ideas, c. 500-1400*, ed. by Claudia Bolgia, Rosamond McKitterick and John Osborne, Cambridge, Cambridge University Press, 2011, pp. 305-322.

exceptional the accounts of Gerald, Gervase and Gregory actually are. It is also instructive to review and compare their experiences of, and attitudes to, ancient Rome and antiquity, to see if they share a consistent insular view of the ancient past. Before that, however, we should consider the conceptual tools and heuristic methods our insular authors brought to their Roman experience.

2. Texts and Authors

We encounter Gerald of Wales as a fully-formed author well before his first visit to Rome. He was extremely well-read in the classics, although his citations prove that he was accustomed to quote from manuals as well as from a well-stocked memory.[1] Although his Latin style was less pyrotechnic than that of his friend Walter Map, it was polished and resilient, and he was acutely sensitive to the part eloquence played in dignifying its subject matter: "Let us follow the example of great orators, who, in an admirable manner, most polished the shafts of their eloquence, when the poverty of their subject required it to be elevated by the superiority of their style".[2] In fact, Gerald's early writings drew an approving comment from no less an exacting critic than Francesco Petrarch.[3]

Gerald was also an extraordinarily perceptive observer in his descriptions of Ireland and Wales. His first book, the *Topographia Hibernica*, contains a description of the birds, animals and miracles of Ireland and was an immediate success.[4] Like the subsequent descriptions of Wales, it was accessibly written and aimed at the widest audience.

Gerald also described, as a competent and credible ear-witness, Welsh singers and their musical performance techniques, and earlier in the *Topographia Hibernica* he commented on Irish harp-playing and the harpist's techniques: "It is remarkable how, in spite of the great speed of the fingers, the musical proportion is maintained. The melody is kept perfect and full with unimpaired art through

1. Bartlett, *Gerald of Wales: A Voice of the Middle Ages*, p. 63; André A. Goddu, Richard H. Rouse, "Gerald of Wales and the Florilegium Angelicum", *Speculum* (1977), pp. 488-491; Simon Meecham-Jones, "Style, Truth and Irony: Listening to the Voice of Gerald of Wales' Writings,' in *Gerald of Wales: New Perspectives*, ed. by Henley and Mullen, pp. 127-144: 130.

2. "Quibus in admirabili genere causae acuenda praecipue sunt arma facundae, ut exilitatem materiae gravior stilus atollat", in Meecham-Jones, "Style, Truth and Irony", p. 134.

3. *Familiarum rerum libri* 3.1.7: "… libellus De mirabilibus Hybernie a Giraldo quodam aulico Henrici secondi regis Anglorum, licet tenui rerum filo, non rudi tamen verborum arte contextus". Ugo Dotti, *Le familiari*, vol. 3, Rome, Archivio Guido Izzi, 1994, p. 6; Robert Bartlett, *Gerald of Wales and the Ethnographic Imagination*, Cambridge, Department of Anglo-Saxon, Norse and Celtic, 2013, p. 5, n. 16.

4. Bartlett, *Gerald of Wales and the Ethnographic Imagination*, p. 4. It was begun before Gerald left Ireland in May 1186 and presented to Archbishop Baldwin in March 1188: Bartlett, *Gerald of Wales: A Voice of the Middle Ages*, p. 174. John J. O'Meara, *Gerald of Wales: The History and Topography of Ireland*, London, Penguin Books, 1982.

everything [...] with a rapidity that charms, a rhythmic pattern that is varied, and a concord achieved through elements discordant".[5] It is clear that Gerald was aware of and proud of his discerning musical taste: "Hence it happens that the very things that afford unspeakable delight to the minds of those who have a fine perception and can penetrate carefully to the secrets of the art, bore, rather than delight, those who have no such perception".[6] His account of Welsh choral music and singing, while not always transparent or easy to understand, is remarkable, and may have been partly informed by knowledge of some manual like Guido of Arezzo's *Micrologus*.[7] Nevertheless, there are moments when one can sense Gerald the ethnographer trying to move beyond the descriptive conventions of elite music in order to record a non-learned musical practice accurately.

It was not only the native fauna that caught his eye. His description of a great masterpiece of insular gospels at Kildare (Fig. 2) in his first work, the *Topographia Hibernica*, is truly astonishing:

> Among all the miracles of Kildare, nothing seems to me more miraculous than that wonderful book which they say was written under the direction of an angel at the time of the Virgin. The book contains the concordance of the four gospels according to Saint Jerome, where for almost every page there are different designs, distinguished by varied colours. Here you may see the face of Majesty divinely drawn, there the mystic symbols of the Evangelists, each with wings, now six, now four, and now two: here you will see the eagle, there the calf; here the man, there the lion, and other forms almost infinite. Look at them superficially with the ordinary casual glance, and you would think it an erasure and not tracery. Fine craftsmanship is all about you, but you might not notice it. Look more keenly at it and you will penetrate to the very shrine of art. You will pick out intricacies, so delicate and subtle, so exact and compact, so full of knots and links, with colours so fresh and vivid, that you might say that all this was the work of an angel and not of man.[8]

5. O'Meara, *History and Topography of Ireland*, p. 103; *GC Opera*, vol. V, *Topographia Hibernica*, ed. by James F. Dimock, London, Longmans, Green, Reader and Dyer, 1867, pp. 153 ff. The passage is repeated verbatim in the *Descriptio Kambriae*. See *The Journey Through Wales and Description of Wales*, ed. by Thorpe, p. 239.

6. Shai Burstyn, "Is Gerald of Wales a Credible Musical Witness?", *The Musical Quarterly*, 72/2 (1986), pp. 155-169: 168. Margaret Bent, "Reading, Memory, Listening, Improvisation: From Written Text to Lost Sound", *Basler Jahrbuch für Historische Musikpraxis*, 34 (2010), pp. 13-28. Translation from O'Meara, *History and Topography of Ireland*, p. 104: "Hinc accidit ut ea, quae subtilius intuentibus, et artis arcana acute discernentibus, internas et ineffabiles comparant animi delicias, ea non attendentibus, sed quasi videndo non videntibus, et audiendo non intelligentibus, aures potius onerent que delectent". See also *GC Opera*, vol. V, p. 154.

7. Burstyn, "Is Gerald of Wales a Credible Musical Witness?", pp. 161-162; Shai Burstyn, "Gerald and the *Sumer* Canon", *Journal of Musicology*, 11 (1983), pp. 135-150.

8. George Henderson, *From Durrow to Kells*, London, Thames and Hudson, 1987, p. 195: "Inter universa Kildariae miracula nihil mihi miraculosius occurrit quam liber ille mirandum, tempore virginis, ut aiunt, angelo dictante conscriptus. Continet hic liber quatuor Evangeliorum juxta Ieronimum concordantium: ubi quot pagina fere tot figurae diversae variisque coloribus distinctissimae. Hic Majestatis vultum videas divinitus impressum; hinc mysticas Evangelistarum formas, nunc senas, nunc quaternas, nunc binas alas habentes; hinc aquilam, inde vitulum, hinc hominis faciem, inde leonis; aliasque figuras fere infinitas. Quas si superficialiter et usuali more minus acute conspexeris, litura potius videbitur quam ligatura; nec ullam prorsus attendes subtilitatem ubi nihil tamen praeter subtilitatem. Sin

Gerald was an unusually perspicacious observer of the natural world. This visual acuity would later also serve him well in his analysis of buildings.

Some five or six years later, he wrote the first version of the *Descriptio Kambriae.*[9] He had been familiar with the Augustinian house at Llanthony from an early date, before it fell within his archdeaconry at Brecon, to such an extent that some have suggested he might have visited when he studied at St Peter's in Gloucester some 50 miles away. It may even be the case that the manuscript of the *History of Llanthony Priory*, now in the British Library, is a late product of his pen, as has recently been argued.[10] He was a supporter of the Augustinian order, in general, and admired their moderation and temperance. They were, in Gerard's opinion, less avaricious than the Cistercians and less given to luxury and excess than the Benedictines.[11]

In his *Itinerary*, Gerald's description of the site of Llanthony is extraordinary in its precision and its evocativeness (Fig. 3):

> In the deep vale of Ewias, which is shut in on all sides by a circle of lofty mountains and which is no more than three arrow shots in width, there stands the abbey church of Saint John the Baptist [...] built on the bank of the Honddu, in a deep recess where that river flows along the vale. It is from the Honddu that it takes the name Llanhonddu, for llan means a place dedicated to religion. It rains a lot there because of the mountains, the winds blow strong, and in winter it is always capped with clouds. The climate is temperate and healthy, the air soothing and clement, if somewhat heavy, and illness is rare. [...] As they sit in their cloisters in this monastery, breathing the fresh air, the monks gaze up at distant prospects which rise above their own lofty roof-tops, and they see, as far as the eye can reach, mountain-peaks that rise to meet the sky and often enough herds of deer that graze on their summits. Even on a clear day, the sun's round ball is not visible above those lofty mountain-tops until the hour of prime, or maybe just before. This formerly was a happy, a delightful spot, most suited to the life of contemplation, a place from its first founding fruitful and to itself sufficient.

This, we should remember, could have been the earlier church on the site, although the third and final recension of the *Itinerarium Kambriae* was

autem ad perspicacius intuendum oculorum aciem invitaveris, et longe penitius ad artis arcana transpenetraveris, tam delicatas et subtiles, tam arctas et artitas, tam nodosas et vinculatim colligatas, tamque recentibus adhuc coloribus illustratas notare poteris intricaturas, ut vere haec omnia potius angelica quam humana diligentia jam asseveraveris esse composita". See *GC Opera*, vol. V, bk 2, ch. 38, p. 123.

9. Bartlett, *Gerald of Wales: A Voice of the Middle Ages*, p. 176 agrees with Dimock that there were two recensions, c. 1194 and c. 1215. Gerald of Wales, *The Journey Through Wales and Description of Wales*, pp. 96-97; Huw Pryce, "Gerald's Journey through Wales", *Journal of Welsh Ecclesiastical History*, 6 (1989), pp. 17-34; Gerd Tellenbach, "Zur Frühgeschichte abendländischer Reisebeschreibungen", in *Historia Integra Festschrift für Erich Hassinger zum 70. Geburtstag*, ed. by Hans Fenske, Wolfgang Reinhard and Ernst Schulin, Berlin, Duncker und Humblot, 1977, pp. 51-80: 55-57.

10. British Library Cotton MS Julius D, x. fols 31-53v. See also Robert Bartlett, "Gerald of Wales and the History of Llanthony Priory", in *Gerald of Wales: New Perspectives*, pp. 81-93.

11. *GC Opera*, vol. VI, p. 41; Gerald of Wales, *The Journey Through Wales and Description of Wales*, pp. 103, 105-106; Bartlett, "Gerald of Wales and the History of Llanthony Priory", p. 88.

(re-)written in 1214.[12] The new church at Llanthony was erected around 1210, and although it was an Augustinian foundation, this second church was related in concept and architectural style to the Cistercian buildings in the West of England.[13] Llanthony also had an imposing double-towered façade, which is now an evocative ruin.

This affectionate and evocative description of the landscape setting of a church is not in itself new in English religious writing. Most famous perhaps is the remarkable vignette, a generation earlier, from the pen of the Cistercian abbot Ailred of Rievaulx (1110-1167), which described the situation of his abbey in the North Riding of Yorkshire:

> The spot was by a powerful stream called the Rie in a broad valley stretching on either side. The name of their little settlement and of the place where it lies was derived from the name of the stream and the valley, Rievaulx. High hills surround the valley, encircling it like a crown. These are clothed by trees of various sorts and maintain in pleasant retreats the privacy of the vale, providing for the monks a kind of second paradise of wooded delight. From the loftiest rocks, the waters wind and tumble down to the valley below, and as they make their hasty way toward the lesser passages and narrower beds and spread themselves in wider rills, they give out a gentle murmur of soft sound and join together in the sweet notes of a delicious melody. And when the branches of lovely trees rustle and sing together and the leaves flutter gently to the earth, the happy listener is filled increasingly with a glad jubilee of harmonious sound, as so many various things conspire together in such a sweet consent, in music whose every diverse note is equal to the rest. His ears drink in the feast prepared for them and are satisfied.[14]

In the case of Llanthony, we can still verify the accuracy of Gerald's observation by visiting the site. The mountains do indeed rise steeply on both sides of the priory, and it would be easy to imagine the religious struggling to read and write there during a 13th-century winter. This is a topographical description of a subjective immediacy that compares well with Ailred's earlier encomium and that has a vitality which exceeds even that of Master Gregory's celebrated appraisal

12. *GC Opera*, vol. VI, pp. xxxiii-xxxix; Bartlett, *Gerald of Wales: A Voice of the Middle Ages*, p. 178.

13. Jean Bony, *French Gothic Architecture of the 12th and 13th centuries*, Berkeley, University of California Press, 1983, p. 439.

14. *Walteri Danielis Vita Ailredi Abbatis Revall'*, ed. by Frederick M. Powicke, London, Thomas Nelson and Sons, 1950, pp. 12-13: "…super validissimum torrentem Rie nomine planicie vallis latissime hinc inde circumiacente casas fixere suas. Habitaculi autem sui nomen et loci eiusdem ex duobus composuerunt,videlicet ex ipsius torrentis vocabulo et valle, unde Rievallis nuncupatur. Quam vallem excelsi montes circumambiunt et instar corone circumcingunt, qui arborea varietate vestiuntur amenisque secessibus vicinia secreta ministrant et monachis nemorose delicie alterum quodammodo exhibent paradisum. Crispantes fontes ex eminentissimis rupibus labuntur ad inferiora vallis dumque per fibras minores et strictiores decurrunt venas terre patulosque rivulos ac rivas prominentes leni murmure suaviter sibilant et sonis dulcibus melos delectabile concinunt. Set et ramosa collisio pulcherimarum arborum foliis in humum convolantibus molli collapsu in carmineos conveniunt (sic) modos fitque gratum audientibus nimis nimisque iocundum iubilum tam concordantis armonie dum perdulci concentu tantarum diversitatum concitatarum ad sonos varios et equipollentes in musica oblectantur aures ebibentes que promuntur…"

of the panorama of Rome, which we will examine in a later chapter. It compares with other landscape passages in Gerald's writings, not least his affectionately evocative description of his boyhood home at Manorbier.

However, this eloquent account of the setting of a remote Augustinian house in no way prepares the reader of the *Itinerarium* for Gerald's even more remarkable forensic description of the ruins of the Roman legionary fortress of Caerleon (Fig. 4). This was Isca, near Newport in South Wales, the garrison of the Second Augustan Legion between the 1st and 3rd centuries CE. Gerald and his companions reached it on Saturday 12 March 1191, and he described it as such:

> Caerleon is the modern name of the City of the Legions. In Welsh *caer* means a city or encampment. The legions sent to this island had the habit of wintering on this spot, and so it came to be called City of the Legions. Caerleon is of unquestioned antiquity. It was constructed with great care by the Romans, the walls being built of brick. You can still see the main vestiges of its one-time splendour. There are immense palaces, which, with the gilded gables of their roofs, once rivalled the magnificence of ancient Rome. They were set up in the first place by some of the most eminent men of the Roman state, and they were therefore embellished with every architectural conceit. There is a lofty tower, and beside it remarkable hot baths, the remains of temples and an amphitheatre. All is enclosed within impressive walls, parts of which still remain standing. Wherever you look, both within and without the circuit of these walls, you can see constructions dug deep into the earth, conduits for water, underground passages and air-vents. Most remarkable of all to my mind are the stoves, which once transmitted heat through narrow pipes inserted in the side-walls, and which are built with extraordinary skill. Caerleon is beautifully situated on the bank of the River Usk. When the tide comes in, ships sail right up to the city.[15]

I know of no other medieval writer who describes ancient Roman domestic architectural structure so penetratingly. Other Roman hypocausts have been revealed by modern excavation and some survive at sites like Arles.[16] In Gerald's writings, he makes no attempt to "domesticate" the strange. There were no

15. Translation from Gerald of Wales, *The Journey Through Wales and Description of Wales*, pp. 114-115, 55. *GC Opera*, vol. VI, pp. 55-56: "...in Novoburgo, ter Oscha flumine jam transcurso pernoctavimus. Dicitur autem Kaerleun Legionum urbs. Kaer enim Britannice urbs vel castrum dicitur. Solent quippe legiones a Romanis in insulam misse, ibi hiemare; et inde Urbs Legionum dicta est. Erat autem haec urbs antiqua et authentica, et a Romanis olim coctilibus muris egregie constructa. Vides hic multa pristinae nobilitatis adhuc vestigia; palatia immensa, aureis olim tectorum fastigiis Romanos fastus imitantia. Eo quod a Romanis principibus primo constructa, et aedificiis egregiis illustrata fuissent; turrim giganteam, thermas insignes, templorum reliquias, et loca theatralia; egregiis muris partim adhuc extantibus omnia clausa. Reperies ubique, tam intra murorum ambitum quam extra, aedificia subterranean, aquarum ductus, hypogeos / 56 que meatus. Et quod inter alia notabile censui, stuphas undique videas miro artificio consertas; lateralibus quibusdam et praeangustis spiraculi viis occulte calorem exhalantibus [...] Situs Urbis egregius, super Oschiae flumen; navigio, mare influente, idoneum". Note the brevity of Gervase: "Caerleim, id est civitatem Legionum; illuc Cesar duodecim legiones in yberna dimisit, que illam civitatem miro opera construxerunt".

16. The amphitheatre at Arles has been attributed to the late Flavian or Trajanic period. See John Ward-Perkins, "Roman Architecture", in *Etruscan and Roman Architecture*, ed. by Axel Boëthius and John Ward Perkins, Harmondsworth, Penguin Books, 1970, p. 353; Marc Heijmans, *Arles durant l'Antiquité tardive de la Duplex Arelas à l'urbs Genesii*, Rome, École Française de Rome, 2004, pp. 139-160.

salmon in his Macedon.[17] Nevertheless, the whole passage reveals Gerald as an inquisitive and analytical observer of the ancient past, well before he wrote the passages in his *Speculum ecclesiae*, to which we shall return later. His remarkable analysis of an ancient insular manuscript in Ireland shows that this visual acumen extended beyond contemporary buildings. The accounts Gerald gives us in both the *Itinerarium Hibernica* and the slightly later the *Itinerarium Kambriae* (*Journey through Wales*) should rightly give us unusual confidence in his Roman observations.

Gerald's description of Caerleon and its Roman hypocausts of 1188 is significantly more detailed than William of Malmesbury's vivid description of a ruinous Roman building at Carlisle in the first part of his *Gesta pontificum Anglorum*, composed some seventy years earlier: "… you may see at Carlisle a *triclinum* vaulted in stone that no violence of the elements, or even the intentional setting alight of the timbers piled up against it, has succeeded in destroying".[18] This is almost trivial in comparison. And in its attitude to the architectural remnants of the past, Gerald is more acute, if less romanticised, than the *The Ruin*, an Anglo-Saxon poem that likely refers to the Roman *Aquae sulis*, an ancient building in Bath:

> This masonry is wondrous; fates broke it
> Courtyard pavements were smashed: the work of giants is decaying
> Roofs are fallen, ruinous towers […]
> Often this wall
> Lichen-grey and stained with red experienced one reign after another
> Remained standing under storms; the high wide gate has collapsed.[19]

Scholars have surmised that Gerald's early ethnographical writings had marginal illustrations to assist the reader.[20] Whether or not this was the case, it is evident that Gerald was acutely aware of the limitations of the written word to convey the fullest meaning to his readers. There is one very suggestive intervention in his *Descriptio Kambriae*. Struggling to describe a specifically Welsh reaping tool, he confesses that a drawing would be helpful for the reader: "They do not usually use sickles when they reap, for they prefer a short piece of iron in the shape of a knife, which is loosely joined to a stick at either end. (As Horace says in his *Ars Poetica*):

17. Fluellen's speech is in *Henry V*, act IV, scene vii.

18. William of Malmesbury, *Gesta Regum anglorum*, ed. by Rodney Thomson and Michael Winterbottom, Oxford, Oxford University Press, 1998, p. 325; Roger S. O. Tomlin, Richard G. Annis, "A Roman Altar from Carlisle Castle", *Transactions of the Cumberland and Westmorland Antiquarian and Archaeological Society*, 89 (1989), pp. 77-92.

19. Anglo-Saxon text in *Three Old English Elegies: The Wife's Lament, The Husband's Message, The Ruin*, ed. by Roy F. Leslie, Manchester, Manchester University Press, 1961; Anne Thompson Lee, "The Ruin: Bath or Babylon? A Non-Archaeological Investigation", *Neuphilologische Mitteilungen*, 74 (1973), pp. 443-455; David R. Howlett, "Two Old English Encomia", *English Studies*, 57 (1976), pp. 289-293.

20. Michelle Brown, "Marvels of the West: Giraldus Cambrensis and the Role of the Author in the Development of Marginal Illustration", *English Manuscript Studies 1100-1700*, 10 (2002), pp. 34-59: 31, 39.

We are more impressed by what our eyes see clear
Than we can ever be by what we hear

If you saw it, you would understand this better than you can hope to do by listening to my description".[21] It was a dilemma shared with other later ethnographically-minded travellers, like the Franciscan Willem van Ruysbroek, who in 1253 lamented his inability to properly describe the painted wagons of the Tartar women:[22] "The women themselves paint very beautiful carts, which I do not know how to describe to you, unless I were to make a picture, if I knew how to paint". It may be that Gerald himself was an illustrator, as has been inferred not only from the *Topographia Hibernica*, but also the lost *Mappa Kambriae*.[23] If so, it was a talent he regrettably neglected in Rome.

Before the Italian Renaissance, however, nothing approaches Gerald's level of archaeological specificity.[24] And the remains at Caerleon, we should bear in mind, were Roman vestiges on the northern frontiers of empire, observed before Gerard had any personal experience of Rome itself. And yet, if Gerald presents the portrait of a landscape with unusual specificity, it is only in these early "ethnographic" landscapes that he places himself and describes his actions.

There is a curious disjunction in all this, which becomes clearer when we examine our individual observer's approach to Rome itself. Gerald, the pioneer ethnographer, had scrutinised the Roman provincial ruins at Caerleon with unsurpassed acumen. Yet, when he arrives in Rome itself and is confronted by far more imposing ruins than could ever have existed at Caerleon, he concentrates his attention on the foundation of the Christian church in the Constantinian period, and his wide classical learning serves only to embellish his prose style and enliven his description of 13th-century Rome rather than to inform his readers

21. Gerald of Wales, *The Journey Through Wales and Description of Wales*, p. 252. *GC Opera*, vol. VI, bk 1, ch. 18: "Falcibus quoque minus utuntur ad metendum: plus autem expeditius ferro quodam modico, in cultelli modum formato, baculis ad capita laxe et flexibiliter catenato. Sed quoniam: 'segnius irritant animos demissa per aures / Quam quae sunt oculis subjecta fidelibus' Melius videndo quam audiendo modum attendes". His quotation, from Horace, *Ars Poetica*, lines 180-181, is evidently from memory, as Gerald gives *aures* for *aurem*.

22. *Sinica Franciscana I Itinera et Relationes Fratrum Minorum saeculi XIII et XIV*, ed. by Anastasius van den Wyngaert O.F.M., Florence, Quaracchi, 1929, and specifically Fr. Guillelmus de Rubruc [William of Rubruck], *Itinerarium Cap. II (De Tartaris et domibus eorum)*, p. 173: "Matrone sibi faciunt pulcherimas bigas, quas nescirem vobis describere, nisi per picturam, immo Omnia depinxissem vobis si scivissem depingere". Bartlett, *Gerald of Wales: A Voice of the Middle Ages*, p. 158 was the first to make this comparison.

23. "Kambriae totius Mappam, cum montanis arduis et silvis horridis, aquis et fluviis et castellis erectis, cathedralibus etiam ecclesiis et monasteriis multis, maximeque Cisterciensis Ordinis copiosa et artificiosa sumptuositate constructis, arcto folio, strictoque valde locello et spatio brevissimo distincte tamen et aperto declaravi". The lost map is mentioned in *GC Opera*, vol. I, pp. 414-415; Bartlett, *Gerald of Wales: A Voice of the Middle Ages*, p. 179 dates it after 1220. James Conway Davies, "The Kambriae Mappa of Giraldus Cambrensis", *Journal of the Historical Society of the Church in Wales*, 2 (1952), pp. 46-60; Brown, "Marvels of the West", p. 39: "Gerald's habit of presenting or circulating his works may have led him to produce or commission illustrated copies".

24. I have benefited here from conversations with Howard Burns.

of what he actually observed. In the *Itinerarium Kambriae*, there is a curious account of the emperor Constantine, who had planned to rebuild Troy but then instantly changed course upon hearing a divine premonition that he was about to rebuild Sodom, at which point he turned towards Byzantium, which he rebuilt and to which he attached his name.[25] But, fundamentally, Gerald's attitude to the natural world had changed, whether from frustrated ambition or a shift in psychological approach.[26] Certainly, the brilliant observation of the natural world that distinguished his accounts of both Ireland and Wales became markedly less prominent. It has been suggested, plausibly enough, that it was his embittered retreat from the court of Henry II and wounded vanity that brought about this sea-change.[27] But, fundamentally, it is an alien landscape and he does not rise, as in his earlier writings, to the task of portraying it. Nor, remarkably enough, given his well-informed and lively musical interests, does he comment on the venerable Roman traditions of liturgical singing, which he must have experienced on his visits to the great basilicas in the city.

Yet to ascribe the change in approach so simply to wounded vanity is probably to misconceive it. One innovative aspect of Gerald's early writing is not only its scientific and ethnographic bent, but the fact that the descriptions of Ireland and Wales were penned by an author who had been trained and polished in the Parisian schools. These texts were dissimilar from anything that was being written by contemporary scholastic authors.[28] They are powerfully reminiscent of the insular tradition of scientific writing, which was a characteristic of 12th-century England. It was a tradition from which the celebrated Bishop of Lincoln, Robert Grosseteste, emerged a few years afterwards. It was partially centred around the cathedral of Hereford, situated on the borders of Wales, and a remarkable intellectual centre in this period, which had tried to tempt Gerald to join its chapter.[29] The approach failed, but Hereford instead managed to attract Grosseteste, for whom Gerald himself provided a cordial reference in 1194 or 1195.[30] But Gerald's intellectual development was taking another path. He increasingly preferred to expand and add an allegorical interpretation to his naturalistic observations. It was both easier and evidently impressed more readers. His brilliant visual description of ospreys fishing in Ireland – a sea eagle virtually unknown to either the ancient natural scientists or to the compilers of bestiaries – is vitiated, and even distorted, by an

25. Gerald of Wales, *The Journey Through Wales and Description of Wales*, p. 264; *GC Opera*, vol. VI, p. 215.

26. Bartlett, *Gerald of Wales and the Ethnographic Imagination*, p. 18 attributes the change to his disappointment at Henry II's court. Richard Southern, *Robert Grosseteste: The Growth of an English Mind in Mediaeval Europe*, 2nd ed., Oxford, Oxford University Press, 1992, pp. 99-100. Southern's explanation carries more conviction.

27. Bartlett, *Gerald of Wales: A Voice of the Middle Ages*, pp. 111-127: "The retreat from naturalism". Ian Short, "Literary Culture at the Court of Henry II", in *Henry II: New Interpretations*, ed. by Christopher Harper-Bill and Nicholas Vincent, Woodbridge, Boydell and Brewer, 2007, pp. 335-361.

28. Southern, *Robert Grosseteste*, p. li.

29. *Ibid.*, pp. liii-liv.

30. *GC Opera*, vol. I, p. 249; Southern, *Robert Grosseteste*, p. 65.

attempt to moralise.[31] But what is particularly striking is that this shift from close observation of the natural world to a more allegorising or theological approach can also be observed shortly afterwards in a far greater scholar and younger contemporary of Gerald, Robert Grosseteste himself.[32]

Gervase of Tilbury's reaction to Rome is much more pragmatic: he too gives measurements, or records the exact number of steps inside the Column of Trajan. But a good deal of his information on the monuments and topography of Rome is drawn directly from earlier guide-books, such as the *Mirabilia urbis Romae*.[33] In the same way, his cursory mention of Caerleon was corroborated by a citation from Geoffrey of Monmouth.[34] The *Otia Imperialia* was intentionally encyclopaedic, although with a deliberately light touch. It certainly had a far wider circulation than the writings of any of our other visitors. It was translated into French by Jean d'Antioche for Jean d'Acre. Later still, it merited an approving comment from none other than Giovanni Boccaccio in his *Genealogia deorum*.[35] Yet nowhere does it show either the intellectual curiosity or topographical command that would support the attribution to Gervase, as is sometimes claimed, of the Ebsdorf world map.[36]

With Master Gregory, we remain largely in the dark: little more than his name is known with certainty. This information comes from his own introduction, where he disarmingly presents himself: "Here begins Master Gregory's prologue concerning the wonders which once were or still are in Rome...".[37] That is all. The

31. *GC Opera*, vol. V, bk 1, ch. 16, pp. 49-50: "So does our old enemy see with his sharp glance whatever secret thing we do in the troubled waves of the world". O'Meara, *History and Topography of Ireland*, p. 43. Southern, *Robert Grosseteste*, pp. 99-100: "it was much more difficult and seemed much less useful to see things correctly than to invent moral interpretations of things imperfectly seen".

32. Southern, *Robert Grosseteste*, pp. 135-136.

33. Gervase of Tilbury, *Otia Imperialia*, p. 262, n. 35.

34. *Ibid.*, p. 374: "Caerleim, id est civitatem Legionum; illuc Cesar duodecim legiones in yberna dimisit, que illam civitatem miro opera construxerunt". Gervase's source is Geoffrey of Monmouth. See *Historia Regum Britanniae*, ed. by Acton Griscom, London, Longman, Green & Co., 1929, ch. 44.

35. Gervase of Tilbury, *Otia Imperialia*, p. 28; Boccaccio, *De genealogia deorum*, vii.25 lxxxvi. 12: "Quia igitur optimum nature fatigate remedium amare novitates et gaudere variis...".

36. Jerzy Strzelczyk, *Gerwasy z Tilbury Studium z dziejów uczoności geograficznej w średniowieczu*, Warsaw, Zakład Narodowy im Ossolińskich, 1970, p. 277. Armin Wolf, "Ikonologie der Ebstorfer Weltkarte und politische Situation des Jahres 1239 Zum Weltbild des Gervasius von Tilbury am welfischen Hofe", in *Ein Weltbild vor Columbus. Die Ebstorfer Weltkarte. Interdiziplinäres Kolloquium*, ed. by Hartmut Kugler and Eckhard Michael, Weinheim, VCH Acta Humaniora, 1988, pp. 54-119. Hartmut Kugler, Sonja Glauch, Antje Wittig, *Die Elbstorfer Weltkarte*, Berlin, Akademie, 2007; Gervase of Tilbury, *Otia Imperialia*, p. xxxvi considers the identification of Gervase of Tilbury as Gervase of Ebstorf to be unlikely. Paul D. A. Harvey, *Mappa Mundi: The Hereford World Map*, Hereford, Hereford Cathedral, 2001, p. 56 also leaves the question of identity open. For Gerald's map of Wales, see p. 25, n. 23.

37. *Master Gregorius: The Marvels of Rome*, ed. by Osborne, p. 17. Nardella, *Il fascino*, p. 144: "Incipit prologus magister Gregorius de mirabilibus que quondam fuerunt vel adhuc..."; Étienne Wolff, "Un voyageur à Rome au XII-XIII siècle: Magister Gregorius", *Bulletin de l'Association Guillaume Budé*, 1 (2005) pp. 163-171.

rest remains hypothesis and what can be inferred from his text. Yet here we find, more fully perhaps than in any other 13th-century text, the description of ancient ruins and the sculptures that can still be observed there. In Master Gregory's account, we have a portrait of his Roman surroundings, but, in contrast to Gerald, we have virtually no sense of the author himself. He allows us to capture his personal view of Rome's classical ruins, but we flounder when we enquire how he might have arrived at these insights. One might speculate that the time he was able to devote to discussions with cardinals, and his three visits to his favourite ancient statue, indicate that Gregory had time on his hands, perhaps like those pilgrims who wrote descriptions of Venice while waiting for an appropriate galley to transport them to the Holy Land, or like the petitioners at the papal court, kicking their heels in anticipation of a curial decision, who wrote to their superiors at home.[38] Gregory found an illuminating alternative purpose for his sojourn.

38. I owe this suggestion to Ingo Herklotz.

3. Why Did They Go?

What prompted these remarkable men to make their strenuous and dangerous journeys to Rome? In the case of Gerald, who travelled there most often, iteration was clearly fuelled by grievance. He was convinced that he had been betrayed by his enemies and unjustly cheated of the bishopric of St David's. He was, rather more altruistically, concerned about what he regarded as the distortions of the hierarchy of the church in Wales. He went to Rome to plead, to display his considerable learning with polished mundanity, and, crucially, to find there the vital documentary precedents to buttress his claims. These could only be found in the papal registers.

Pursuit of a legal dispute at the papal curia between the Abbey of Evesham and Bishop Mauger of Worcester (1199-1212) was also the dynamic that brought Thomas of Marlborough to Rome for his lengthy and almost ruinously expensive sojourn between 1204 and 1206. Thomas of Marlborough was a graduate of Oxford University, and also a pupil of Stephen Langton.[1] While at the curia, he even took time off to improve his grasp of the case through a brief refresher course in law at the University of Bologna.[2] Gervase was almost certainly in Rome as a courtier, a member of the imperial entourage, intent on entertaining his master. Among all this, Master Gregory once again proves exceptional. He had access to cardinals, at times clearly on an informal and conversational basis, but his status and the purpose of his visit remain uncertain.[3] Given the quality of his written Latin and hints at legal scholarship, it is probably safest to regard him as a proctor or a similar kind of official representing an East Anglian bishopric at the curia. If we are correct in identifying Gregory with the chancellor to the legate Cardinal Ottone di Tonengo during his legation to England, this would help confirm his

1. Christopher Holdsworth, "Langton, Stephen (c. 1150-1228)", in *Dictionary of National Biography*, vol. XXXII, Oxford, Oxford University Press, 2004, pp. 516-521: 516.

2. Thomas of Marlborough, *History of the Abbey of Evesham*, pp. 275, 311.

3. Talking of the bronze equestrian statue of Marcus, he lets slip "...quam a senioribus et cardinalibus et viris doctissimis didici"; Nardella, *Il fascino*, p. 148. The suggestion that he might have travelled to Rome at the instance of Archbishop Thomas Becket made by Colin Higgins, Kat. n. 51, *Narracio de Mirabilibus Urbis*, Cambridge, St. Catherine's College MS 3 (E.4.96), in *Wunder Roms im Blick des Nordens von der Antike bis zur Gegenwart*, ed. by Christoph Stiegmann, Imhof Peterberg, 2017, pp. 358-360: 359 lacks any foundation.

literary accomplishments. But, although himself admitting to the title of *magister*, he never makes mention of the reason for his stay in Rome.

But the exceptional nature of Gregory's *Narracio* underlines its singularity in another way. While it is the most detailed of our insular observers' descriptions of Rome, it nevertheless lacks a comparative dimension.[4] Nowhere does Gregory offer a domestic analogy for the buildings and artefacts he describes. Gerald and Gervase are similarly deficient, although the latter offers more comparisons. This lacuna may perhaps best be explained by the nature of each account and the dynamic behind it. Gervase and Gerald were not in Rome to share their practical and visual experiences with others. But this answer will not do for Gregory, and, indeed, it goes against the grain of many medieval travel accounts, which are often at pains to domesticate the strange by stressing the similarities of what they see with monuments with which they could safely assume their readers were familiar.[5]

Not every road from England necessarily led to Rome. Two Irish Franciscans, Symon Simeonis and Hugo Illuminator, set out for the Holy Land in March 1323 "seraphicis inflammati ardoribus" ("inflamed with seraphic ardour").[6] Passing through London, "the most famous and wealthy city under the sun", the two friars moved on to Canterbury, where Becket's shrine, "all of gold and adorned with innumerable precious stones and pearls, glittering like a gate of Jerusalem and even crowned by an imperial crown", captured their attention.[7] Paris, like London, was furnished "in a wonderful manner with monasteries and monks and churches with lofty steeples and bell-towers and other beauties of church architecture". They also provided succinct descriptions of Notre Dame and Sainte Chapelle.[8] Eventually they reached Venice and remarked on San Marco, "incomparably

4. Maurizio Campanelli, "Monuments and Histories: Ideas and Images of Antiquity in Some Descriptions of Rome", in *Rome across Time and Space*, pp. 35-51.

5. Ludolf von Sudheim is always keen to offer comparisons with Paderborn or Osnabrück: *Ludolphi rectoris ecclesiae parochialis in Suchem de itinere Terra Sanctae liber*, Stuttgart, Litterarischer Verein, 1851, pp. 77, 95. Burchard of Mount Sion remarked that the neck of a giraffe he had seen was so long that it could lick the vault of the Dominican church at Magdeburg; Jonathan Rubin, "Burchard of Mount Sion's Descriptio Terrae Sanctae: A Newly Discovered Extended Version", *Crusades*, 13 (2014), pp. 173-190: 184.

6. This is probably a recollection of the *seraphicis desideriorum ardoribus* from the *Legenda Trium Sociorum*, p. 69, which would naturally occur to a Franciscan author. For the text, see Théodore Desbonnets, "Legenda Trium Sociorum, Édition critique", *Archivium Franciscanum Historicum*, 67 (1974), pp. 38-144: 87. A composition date of 1246 is probable. *Itinerarium Symonis Semeonis ab Hybernia ad Terram Sanctam*, *Scriptores Latini Hiberniae*, vol. IV, ed. by Mario Esposito, Dublin, Dublin Institute for Advanced Studies, 1960, p. 24.

7. *Itinerarium Symonis Semeonis*, p. 26: "Quod est in in monasterio Nigrorum Monachorum, sub capsa ex auro purissimo mirifice fabrefacta et lapidibus pretiosis innumerabilibus, margaritis nitentibus velut porta Jerusalem ac gemmis choruscantibus inestimabiliter ornate ac etiam imperiali dyademate coronate".

8. *Ibid.*, p. 30: "…ecclesia ex lapidibus sectis et scultpis in honore Virginis Marie constructa, consistit cujus porte occidentales nimia varietate sculpturarum atque turrium altitudine decorantur. […] pulcherrima atque famosa cappella biblicism historiis mirabiliter ornate, In qua sunt pretiossissime reliquie…".

adorned with wonderful mosaic work of Biblical scenes and the adjoining Piazza, the like of which is nowhere to be found".[9] The Irish friars seem deliberately to have chosen a route that avoided Rome.

Another anonymous English Franciscan, who made the pilgrimage to Jerusalem around 1344/1345, visited the Eternal City on his outward journey. After having encountered an estimated 20,000 pilgrims returning from Rome en route, he reached the city and went immediately to Saint Peter's, "the mistress of all churches". It had five aisles and the scale of the nave impressed him deeply: it was, he estimated, as long as a crossbow shot: "It is so spacious that if you lose your companion within it, you would seek him in the crowds of worshippers for a whole day".[10] Our unknown Englishman, like his Irish *confrères*, had no reason to visit the papal curia. Yet these are topographical descriptions of an articulateness and vivacity that the 12th-century visitors could not yet match.

What did our earlier visitors expect to encounter when they came to the curia? To an extent, the papal court resembled the secular courts with which our travellers were, in varying degrees, familiar.[11] Gerald and Gervase were seasoned courtiers. It was a great household, like that of Henry II, and it also included a *camera*, a chancery and a chapel. Innocent III directed his chancery with an autocratic hand, and during his pontificate it expanded hugely in personnel and organisational complexity. For the first seven years of his pontificate, he left the office of chancellor unfilled, doubtless because he wished to have direct control of his chancery. He instated fixed fees for curial scribes and instituted public audiences where the letters were read aloud or amended before dispatch.[12] Innocent was by nature a codifier, a classifier and an active declarator of canon law. His curia was pre-eminently a court of justice where ecclesiastics commonly

9. *Ibid.*, p. 34: "In honore autem predicti evangeliste est ecclesia sumptiossisima, et incomparabiliter lapidibus marmoreis ac aliis pretiossimis constructa, et biblicism historris opera musaico excellenter ornate atque pulcrificata".

10. Girolamo Golubovich, *Biblioteca bio-bibliografica della Terra Santa e dell'Oriente Francescana*, vol. IV, Quaracchi, Typog. Franciscana, 1923, pp. 427-460: 441, "Octavo die mensis novembris incipiente [...] venimus Romam, et incontinenti ivimus ad ecclesiam sancti Petri, omnium ecclesiarum magistram,que est citra Tyberim, quasi in Angulo civitatis, in quodam loco multum elevato: ad illam ascenditur per plures gradus [...] omnium ecclesiarum mundi contentissima; quinque tecta et quatuor columpnarum ordines, duecentos pedes in latum et quantum iaceret ballista in longum, ut estimo...". Eugene Hoade, *Western Pilgrims: The Itineraries of Fr. Simon Fitzsimons (1322-23), a Certain Englishman (1344-45), Thomas Byng (1392) and Notes on Other Authors and Pilgrims*, Jerusalem, Franciscan Press, 1952, p. 53.

11. Malcolm Vale, *The Princely Court Medieval Courts and Culture in North-West Europe*, Oxford, Oxford University Press, 2001, pp. 16-17, 21, 22; Peter Dinzelbacher, *Structures and Origins of the Twelfth-Century "Renaissance"*, Stuttgart, Anton Hiersemann, 2017, pp. 269-279. See p. 14 above.

12. Patrick Zutshi, "Innocent III and the Reform of the Papal Chancery", in *Innocenzo III Urbis et Orbis. Atti del Congresso internazionale (Roma, 9 – 15 settembre 1998)*, ed. by Andrea Sommerlechner, Rome, 2003, vol. I, pp. 84-101: 85-87; Peter Herde, *Audientia Litterarum Contradictarum Untersuchungen über die päpstlichen Justizbreve und die päpstliche Delegationsgerichtsarkeit vom 13. bis zum Beginn des 16. Jahrhunderts*, Tübingen, Niemeyer, 1970, vol. I, pp. 20-21.

went to have their problems and grievances resolved. They might go there of their own accord or have been summoned by the pontiff to justify their actions or conduct.

Resemblances could have two sides. Many members of the papal curia would have instantly recognised, and perhaps concurred, with Walter Map's strikingly negative definition of the English court. Walter, like Gerald, with whom he was surely acquainted, originated from the Welsh marches and became archdeacon of Oxford in 1197.[13] His description is exemplary:

> "In time I exist, and of time I speak" said Augustine, and added, "What time it is I know not. In a similar spirit of perplexity, I may say that in the court I exist, and of the court I speak, and what the court is, God knows, I know not. I do know, however, that the court is not time; but temporal it is, changeable and various, space-bound and wandering, never continuing in one state. When I leave it, I know it perfectly: when I return, I find nothing, or but little of what I left there. I am become a stranger to it, and it to me. […] We courtiers are assuredly a number, and an infinite one, striving to please one individual. But today we are one number, tomorrow we shall be a different one: yet the court is not changed; it remains always the same".[14]

Walter, although a courtier, was mockingly inquisitive. His brief and probably incomplete treatise is now generally entitled *De nugis curialium* ("The Trifles of a Courtier"), and it was composed between 1180 and 1193.[15] As far as we know, however, Walter's text remained largely unknown throughout the medieval period. Like the English royal court, the curia was itinerant; the pope generally spent the summer months outside Rome, during the first half of the 13th century mainly in Campagna to the south, and in the second half, with the arrival of the French papacy, in small towns north of Rome, like Viterbo, Orvieto or Perugia.[16]

13. A. Keith Bate, "Walter Map and Giraldus Cambrensis", *Latomus*, 31 (1972), pp. 860-875: 860-863, 872 is sceptical of their friendship. See also Tony Davenport, "Sex, Ghosts and Dreams: Walter Map (1135? – 1210?) and Gerald of Wales (1146-1223)", in *Writers of the Reign of Henry II: Twelve Essays*, ed. by Ruth Kennedy and Simon Meecham-Jones, New York, Palgrave, 2006, pp. 133-150; Joshua B. Smith, *Walter Map and the Matter of Britain*, University Park, University of Pennsylvania Press, 2017.

14. Walter Map, *De Nugis Curialium: Courtiers' Trifles*, ed. and transl. by Montague R. James, rev. by Christopher N. L. Brooke and Roger A. B. Mynors, Oxford, Oxford University Press, 1983, p. 2: "In tempore sum et de tempore loquor, ait Augustinus et adiecit: nescio quid sit tempus. 'Ego simili possum admiracione dicere quod in curia sum, et de curia loquor, et nescio, Deus scit, quid scit curia… Scio tamen quod curia non est tempus; temporalis quidem est, mutabilis et varia, localis et erratica, nunquam in eodem statu permanens. In recessu meo totam agnosco, in reditu nichil aut modicum invenio quod dereliquerim; extraneam video factus alienus. Eadem est curia, sed mutata sunt membra". Bate, "Walter Map and Giraldus Cambrensis", p. 875 suggests that Gerald knew the text and plagiarised it in *De principis instructione*.

15. Bate, "Walter Map and Giraldus Cambrensis", pp. 867-868; Lewis Thorpe, "Walter Map and Gerald of Wales", *Medium Aevum*, 47/1 (1978), pp. 6-21: 13; Andreas Bihrer, "Selbstvergewisserung am Hof. Eine Interpretation von Walter Maps 'De nugis curialium' I 1-12", *Jahrbuch für internationale Germanistik*, 34 (2002), pp. 227-258.

16. Paravicini Bagliani, "La mobilità della Curia Romana", in *Itineranza pontificia*, pp. 155-278.

The papal archive nevertheless appears to have remained in Rome. It was there that Gerald was able to gain access in his search for historical documentation on the historical status of the see of St David's. He was allowed to consult the register of Eugenius III (1145-1153), but only under strict surveillance. In the second *Distinctio* of his *De jure et statu Menevensis ecclesiae*, he tells of his experience. A cleric from the papal chamber sat beside him the entire time, hawk-eyed. Once he had found the crucial passage he asked for, and was given permission to transcribe it, "Adjecit tamen et supplicavit, quatinus registri Eugenius III papae, [...] quo impetrato [...] coram cleric camerarii consedente et totum observante, confestim invenit [...] Eas enim archidiaconus a camerario licentia data statim transcribere fecit".[17] Innocent III was taking the precautions that had become necessary; he was still furious with a Hungarian cleric, who, shortly prior, had been allowed to consult another recent register, that of Alexander III (1159-1181), and who had simply abstracted the entry from the relevant volume. Nonetheless, an aside from Gervase suggests that he, too, had access to papal documents, for he mentions a list of bishoprics that he had drawn up after a visit to the archives.[18]

These three learned men were not the only British visitors to Rome in the early 13th century. A useful control, as we have seen, is provided by the account of Thomas of Marlborough, the proctor of the distinguished exempt abbey of Evesham in its violent conflict with the overbearing claims, as the monks saw it, of Bishop Mauger of Worcester.[19] Thomas was there to plead a legal case, and Rome was where the action was. In general, as Christopher Cheney remarked, "English abbeys were not anxious to wash their dirty linen in the Tiber: the laundry was expensive and did not always wash clean".[20] Although Thomas' lively account of his visit and encounters with Innocent III is very revealing, it is devoid of local topographical detail. Of our English visitors to Rome, Thomas of Marlborough is the exception in coming with halting feet, in the fervent hope that his slightly shaky case would succeed.

Thomas was an erudite man who had grown up in the shadow of Cardinal Stephen Langton, who may well have present at the curia during several of the visits that interest us. William of Andres met the archbishop-elect when he visited the curia at Viterbo and was impressed by his learning and humility.[21] Langton

17. *GC Opera*, vol. III, p. 180.

18. Gervase of Tilbury, *Otia Imperialia*, p. 218: "Est ergo ordo talis ut ex archivis domini pape collegi".

19. Alain Boureau, "How Law Came to the Monks: The Use of Law in English Society at the Beginning of the Thirteenth Century", *Past and Present*, 167 (2000), pp. 29-74; Amy Locke, "The Abbey of Evesham", in *The Victoria County History of the County of Worcester*, vol. II, ed. by John W. Willis-Bund and William Page, London, Archibald Constable, 1906, pp. 112-119. For Mauger, see Mary G. Cheney, in *Dictionary of National Biography*, vol. XXXVII, Oxford, Oxford University Press, 2004, pp. 414-415.

20. Christopher Cheney, *Pope Innocent III and England*, Stuttgart, Hiersemann, 1976, p. 225; Boureau, "How Law Came to the Monks", pp. 50-53.

21. *Willelmi Chronica Andrensis*, p. 738: "...moribus ornatum, litteris apprime eruditum"; William of Andres, *The Chronicle of Andres*, p. 187.

had studied in Paris and taught at the University of Oxford.[22] Thomas travelled to Rome in 1204 to bring the monks' case forward. Afterwards, writing for his monks at Evesham, Thomas described the curia thus: "...the custom for the Roman curia, like a good mother to console by suckling, if she can, those whom a father's stick has harmed. Hence cases which are being pleaded in the curia, like our case was, are often divided up so that sentence may be pronounced on each part, and no party may depart in sorrow".[23] These are the sentiments of a grateful winner.

It is a classic account of the perils and thrills in the cockpit that was the curia. Innocent III came to appreciate Thomas, and indeed sent him presents of game from the papal hunt.[24] Thomas' mission was greatly complicated by the fact that his sworn enemy, the ruffianly Abbot of Evesham Roger Norreys, who was ultimately ejected by his monks, was opposing him in Rome at the same time.[25] Acting on the advice of the pope and his nephew, cardinal Ugolino Conti (the future Gregory IX), Thomas spent the bulk of 1205 at the University of Bologna, improving his legal expertise and consulting great experts like Azo.[26] Most importantly, however, he had learned how to handle the mercurial pope.

Thomas now knew that Innocent appreciated brevity in pleas.[27] His eyewitness account is peppered with expressions of delight when the abbot's proctor Roger of Clipstone bored the exasperated pope into telling him that he had drunk too much English beer to offer a sensible legal opinion: "Certe et tu et magistri tui multum bibistis de cervisia Anglicana quando hec didicistis".[28] The English proctor

22. Langton was made cardinal-priest of San Crisogono by Innocent III in 1206; he died on 9 July 1228. Werner Maleczek, *Papst und Kardinalskolleg von 1191 – bis 1214, Publikationen des Historischen Instituts beim Oesterreichischen Kulturinstitut in Rom, 1. Abt. Bd.6*, Vienna, Österreichischen Akademie der Wissenschaften, 1984 pp. 164-166. The other contemporary English cardinal was Robert Courson, a Derbyshire man and another pupil of Peter the Chanter. He was made cardinal-priest of Santo Stefano al Celio in 1212 and died at Damietta during the Fifth Crusade on 6 February 1219; Maleczek, *Papst und Kardinalskolleg*, pp. 175-179.

23. "Hec ideo vobis dixerim, quia mos curie Romane est ut pie matris, ut si quos virga patris leserit eosdem uberibus matris si fieri potest consoletur"; Thomas of Marlborough, *History of the Abbey of Evesham*, pp. 426-427; Robert Brentano, *Two Churches: England and Italy in the Thirteenth Century*, Princeton, Princeton University Press, 1968, p. 17; Sayers, "English Benedictine Monks at the Papal Court", pp. 109-129.

24. Thomas of Marlborough, *History of the Abbey of Evesham*, p. 345: "Dum hec agerentur bis intra natiuitatem Domini misit michi dominus papa xenia de uenatione sua".

25. Gervase of Canterbury gives a damning assessment of his character: "Erat enim ab adolescentia monachatus sui superbus, elatus, pomposus in verbis, dolosus in factis, cupidus praelationis, ad superiores adulator, ad inferiores contempnor, gloriosus in veste, negligens in ordinis observatione, amicus foeminarum, amator equorum, iracundus ad correctiones, paratus ad detractiones, in omnibus enim incorrigibilis". *The Historical Works of Gervase of Canterbury*, vol. I, *The Chronicle of the Reigns of Stephen, Henry II, and Richard I*, ed. by William Stubbs, London, Longman & Co., 1879, p. 382.

26. Thomas of Marlborough, *History of the Abbey of Evesham*, p. 276.

27. *Ibid.*, p. 286: "cognoscens quique curia breviloquio gaudebat". Boureau, "How Law Came to the Monks", pp. 61-66.

28. "Then you and your masters had been drinking too much of your English beer when you were learning"; Robert Brentano, *Rome before Avignon*, New York, Basic Books, 1974, p. 153. Thomas of Marlborough, *History of the Abbey of Evesham*, p. 354.

Thomas deeply admired the pope. He recorded his jokes approvingly.[29] Yet he confessed to a cold dread when Innocent closely examined an ancient document he had brought with him to buttress his case, of which authenticity he was, to put it charitably, uncertain.

Thomas had every right to be worried. A case-record of 1199 included in the *Decretals* of Gregory IX demonstrates how scrupulously the authenticity of a submitted document might be assessed by the curia. The document in question was central to a dispute between Filippo da Lampugnano, Archbishop of Milan (1196-1207), and the Benedictine abbey of San Donato at Sesto Calende near Varese, founded in the 9th century by Liutard, Bishop of Pavia between 840 and 864.[30] This is what the curia's investigators reported:

> The false seal appears badly attached. The central figure wears a cap not a mitre and is not clothed in pontifical vestments but imperial robes and holds in his hand not an episcopal crozier, but a sort of sceptre [...] It appears to be an imperial seal, not an episcopal one, which shows the image of Caesar and in the missing half one presumes either his consort or his children. Only the name appears, with the introductory phrase "Dei gratia". But as the correct name of the bishop should be Liutard, 2 letters are erased – the second which stood between "i" and "t" and the sixth, which stood between "r" and "v", so that if the second letter was "o" and the sixth "i", one would doubtless read Lothar and not Liutard [...] furthermore the wax of the inner part of the seal is very old, whereas the wax surrounding it, placed as if to conserve the seal is modern and soft. When one examines the document very carefully there is a hole in the parchment underneath the old seal and the new wax is glued over it as if to attach the faulty old seal to the charter.[31]

29. Thomas of Marlborough, *History of the Abbey of Evesham*, pp. 286-287: "respondit dominus subridendo nunquam defuit alicui copia advocatorum in curia romana". Iben Fonnesberg-Schmidt, William Kynan Wilson, "Smiling, Laughing, and Joking at Rome: Thomas of Marlborough and Gerald of Wales at the Court of Innocent III", *Papers of the British School at Rome*, 86 (2018), pp. 153-181: 165, n. 40.

30. *Decretalium D. Gregorii Papae IX*, Lib. II, Titulus XXII, *De Fide Instrumentorum*, in *Corpus Iuris Canonici*, ed. by Emil Friedberg, Leipzig, Bernard Tauchnitz, 1881, cols 346-349: 347-348; Angelo Bellini, "L'Abbazia e la Chiesa di S. Donato in Sesto Calende", *Archivio Storico Lombardo*, 52 (1925), pp. 79-129.

31. "Tertio, quia falsum sigillum vitiose videbatur appositum, eo quod a media parte sigilli apparebat quaedam imago, non cum mitra in capite, sed cum pileo, nec induta pontificalibus, sed regalibus indumentis tenens in manu non baculem pastoralem sed quasi sceptrum regale, cuius facies non apparebat integra, sed dimidia, tanquam in illa medietate respiceret aliam mediam, quae tamen tota vacua remanebat. Sed quaedam imago videbatur ex ea fuisse deleta, quia cera in ea parte nec in colore, nec in planicie reliquae parti, similis apparebat. Unde non episcopi, sed imperatoris videbatur fuisse sigillum, quia in una medietate Caesaris imaginem exprimebat et in altera medietate praesumebatur, vel filii vel coniugis imaginem habuisse. Nam et in ipso sigillo nullae aliae litterae apparebant, nisi quae nomen proprium cum hac adiectione: 'Dei gratia', designabant. Sed quum proprium nomen ipsius episcopi fuerit Luitardus, in nomine proprio, quod exprimebat sigillum, deletae fuerant duae literae, secunda quae erat inter 'I' et 't', et sexta, quae fuerat inter 'r' et 'v', ita quod si secunda fuisset 'o' et sexta 'i', procul dubio non Luitardus sed Lotharius legeretur. Quod etiam inde convinci poterat quod secundum dispositionem aliarum literarum inter 'l' et 't' non erat spatium, nisi quod potuisset unam literam continere, quum secundum integritatem huius nominis Luitardus inter 'I' et 't' duae literae sint diversae. Praeterea inter 'r' et 'v' tam modicum erat spatium ut in eo nec haec litera 'd' quae maius occupat spatium, sed haec litera 'i' quae minimum occupat, videretur formata fuisse. Rursus quum cera sigilli ab interiori parte

In the case of Evesham Abbey's jurisdiction, Thomas' opponent had alleged that the documents now before the curia had been brought by a certain Nicholas of Warwick, who was a notorious forger. The self-confident pope "took them into his own hands and pulled between the *bulla* and the document to see if he could separate the bulla from the cord [...then] glanced at these, saying 'I know such privileges well, nor can they be faked' and stated, 'These are authentic' and gave them back to me".[32] Thomas' cold fright at Innocent's rough handling of documents that he himself was half-convinced were forgeries subsided, to be replaced by unbridled relief:[33] "Although", he confided in his *Chronicle*, "I had nothing to be guilty about, I knew that the man who was the bearer of the letters and happened to be an official messenger of the curia was considered a forger; and about the privileges of Pope Constantine I was entirely ignorant".[34] Once they were approved, Thomas was seized with unconfined joy. In fact, Innocent III's self-confidence in his own ability to identify forgeries caused him to miss several sizable flaws in Thomas' plea. The curia was clearly much better equipped to unmask forged seals in Italy than to assess the authenticity of purportedly Constantinian privileges confected in England.[35]

Litigation in Rome was enormously expensive, and Thomas had long exhausted his credit. Dangerously short of cash at the end of his lengthy sojourn,

vetustissima esset, cera quae posita erat ab exteriori parte, quasi ad consevationem sigilli, recens erat et mollis. Quod quum diligenter investigatum fuisset, certo certius est compertum, quod sub vetusto sigillo charta fuerat perforata, et per glutinum novae cerae quae posita fuerat exterius, quasi ad conservationem sigilli vitiose fuit ipsi chartae subiunctum. Eadem falsitatis specie per vitiosam videlicedt appositionem sigilli, cetera fere privilegia Romanorum imperatorum prater privilegium Henrici vel falsa reperta sunt, vel falsata": *Decretalium D. Gregorii Papae IX*, Leipzig, Bernhard Tauchnitz, 1881, Lib. II, Titulus XXII, *De Fide Instrumentorum*.

32. Thomas of Marlborough, *History of the Abbey of Evesham*, pp. 296-298: "Et ille [Robert]: 'Pater sancte, bene dixisset adversarius noster [Thomas] si privilegia, in quibus omnem uim et potestatem alleationum suarum fecit et fundamentum totius cause sue posuit, uera essent, cum sint falsa. / nam carta et stilus, filum et bulla, privilegiorum Constantini penitus in terra nostra ignota sunt. Portitor uero indulgentiarum Clementis et Celestini fuit publicus falsarius Nicholaus de Wareuuich, et ideo eas falsas credimus et hoc idem de aliis dicimus'. Et dominus papa precepit ut exhiberem ea, et exhibui. Et dominus papa propriis manibus tractauit ea, et traxit per bullam et cartam si forte posset bullam a filo amouere.Et diligentissime intuens ea tradidit cardinalibus intuenda; et cum per girum venisset iterum ad dominum papam, ostendens privilegium Constantini dixit, 'Huiusmodi privilegia que vobis ignota sunt, nobis sunt notissima, nec possent falsari', et ostendens indulgentia dixit, 'Iste vere sunt', et restituit mihi omnia".

33. *Ibid.*, p. 299: "Set qualiter michi et ecclesie et cause nostre timuerim cum per girum viderunt privilegia cardinales et cum dominus papa ita dure ea tractavit, supersedeo dicere quia non possem vobis edicere. Quamvis nichil michi conscius essem, tamen scivi quod ille qui habebatur pro falsario, forte quia publicum cursor fuit curie, indulgentiarum portitor fuit; et circa privilegia Constantini omnia michi ignota erant. Set cum approbata fuerunt, inestimabili gaudio repletus sum".

34. *Ibid.*, p. 514.

35. Patrick Zutshi, "Innocent III and the Reform of the Papal Chancery", in *Innocenzo III Urbis et Orbis, Atti del Congresso internazionale (Roma, 9-15 settembre 1998)*, vol. I, ed. by Andrea Sommerlechner, Rome, Istituto storico italiano per il medioevo, 2003, pp. 84-101: 86-92; Spaethen, "Giraldus Cambrensis und Thomas von Evesham", pp. 639-644.

he slunk out of Rome at dawn, unable to afford the customary parting gifts to the pope and the curia, but he returned to Evesham triumphant.[36] His achievement was eventually to gain Thomas the abbacy. As we shall see later, the decorations he introduced at the abbey suggest that he had looked more widely when in Rome than his rather self-absorbed account reveals.[37]

The England from which these individuals, plaintiffs or visitors came was far from unknown in the curia. Innocent III had, as a student at Paris, crossed the Channel to visit the shrine of Thomas Becket in Canterbury cathedral.[38] Stephen Langton, the Archbishop of Canterbury, was one of his cardinals. Recently, the kingdom had become something of an ecclesiastical problem-child, and in 1213 King John made his realm a fief of the church, probably in an effort to save his crown. He received it back from God and the Roman Church *tamquam feodatarius* in return for homage and an onerous yearly financial tribute.[39] Several of Innocent III's cardinals had travelled recently to England, largely prompted by the perilous condition of the English Church under King John. Earlier, royal sanctions had been aimed at preventing the English Church from obeying Innocent's directions. An interdict had been imposed in March, 1208; under Innocent III, an interdict had become a political weapon.[40] There could be no church service save for the baptism of children and to enable penance for those who were dying. Marriage and Christian burial could not take place. There was no celebration of Mass. The English church was now squarely between hammer and anvil. An alleviation of restrictions in late 1212 allowed the *viaticum* to be given to the dying. Yet some slight signs of God's favour endured. Gerald, who appears to have spent the year 1209 at Lincoln, records five miracles that took place at the tomb of St Hugh in the cathedral.[41]

Giovanni da Ferentino, cardinal-deacon of Santa Maria in Via Lata, had visited England in 1206 but did not meet the King.[42] Niccolò, Cardinal-Bishop of Tusculum, in the role of *angelus salutis et pacis*, had spent time in England negotiating with King John during one of the most important legations of Innocent III's pontificate about relaxation of the interdict.[43] Niccolò arrived in September 1213

36. Thomas of Marlborough, *History of the Abbey of Evesham*, p. 376.

37. See pp. 83-85 below.

38. *Willelmi Chronica Andrensis*, p. 738. Helene Tillmann, *Papst Innocenz III*, Bonn, Röhrscheid, 1954, pp. 290-291. Gerald himself wore a Becket reliquary: "signaculis B. Thome a collo suspensis"; *GC Opera*, vol. I, pp. 49, 53. Powicke, "Gerald of Wales", p. 121.

39. Christopher Cheney, "King John and the Papal Interdict", *Bulletin of the John Rylands Library*, 31 (1948), pp. 295-317.

40. *Ibid.*, p. 298; Peter D. Clarke, *The Interdict in the Thirteenth Century*, Oxford, Oxford University Press, 2007, pp. 265, 307.

41. *GC Opera*, vol. VII, *Vita S. Remigii, Vita S. Hugonis*, ed. by James Dimock, London, Longman and Co., 1877, pp. 137-147; Adam of Eynsham, *Magna Vita Sancti Hugonis: The Life of St. Hugh of Lincoln*, vol. II, ed. by Decima Douie and Hugh Farmer, Oxford, Oxford University Press, 1985, p. 232. Nicola Coldstream, "English Decorated Shrine Bases", *Journal of the British Archaeological Association*, 39/1 (1976), pp. 15-34.

42. Christopher Cheney, "John of Ferentino, Papal Legate in England", *English Historical Review*, 76 (1961), pp. 654-656; Maleczek, *Papst und Kardinalskolleg*, pp. 147-148.

43. Cheney, *Pope Innocent III and England.* Nicholas de Romanis arrived in September 1213 and was recalled in December the following year; Maleczek, *Papst und Kardinalskolleg*,

but was recalled just over a year later, the following December. He paid a visit to the Abbey of Evesham, where Thomas recorded a brief exchange with him in the chapterhouse on English liturgical practice.[44] Hard on his heels, Guala Bicchieri reached England in May 1216 to support John, now a vassal of the Roman Church, in the dual crises of civil war and French invasion, and to ensure the loyalty of the English Church. He negotiated a peace and swiftly assumed a dominant position in English politics. Thomas of Marlborough spoke of his legal learning with warm admiration.[45] The Cardinal lent his delegated papal authority to Henry III's coronation at St Peter's abbey at Gloucester on 28 October 1216: "...per manus domini G[uala] titulo sancti Martini presbiteri cardinalis [...] invocata spiritus sancti gratia puplice fuimus in regem Anglie inuncti et coronati".[46] Later still, Cardinal Ottone da Tonengo, the probable employer of Magister Gregorius, served as legate between 1237 and 1241.[47]

Thomas did not share the Archdeacon Gerald's evident pleasure in once again hobnobbing with his Parisian university contemporaries and making the pope smile with his witticisms. On his first meeting with Innocent in 1199, he excused the smallness of his gift with a graceful pun. Unlike others, Gerald presented the pontiff with bound copies of his own writings rather than money: *Praestant vobis alii libras, sed nos libros.* Innocent, who Gerald noted approvingly, was *copiose literatus*, appeared delighted by the gift and kept the books – so Gerald claimed – on his bed-side table for months. Of them, the pope's preferred volume was the *Gemma ecclesiastica*.[48]

pp. 147-150; Pietro Silanos, "Niccolò Chiaramonti", *Dizionario Biografico degli Italiani*, vol. LXXVIII, Rome, Istituto della Enciclopedia italiana, 2013, pp. 385-387; Bernard Barbiche, "Les 'diplomates' pontificaux du moyen âge tardif à la première modernité", in *Offices et Papauté (XIVe – XVIIe siècle). Charges, hommes, destins*, ed. by Armand Jamme and Olivier Poncet, Rome, École Française de Rome, 2005, pp. 357-370: 367-368.

44. Thomas of Marlborough, *History of the Abbey of Evesham*, pp. 444-446: "Pater sancte, cum secundum traditionem nostrum non liceat nobis absque femoralibus missas celebrare, et multi ex nobis eodem caveant vestimento, ob defectum eorum multorum sacramentorum celebratio est omissa, quorum numerum propter multitudinem ignore".

45. *Ibid.*, p. 345. Thomas recalled an audience with Innocent III in 1206: "Tunc precepit dominus papa quod recederemus, et post paucos dies dedit nobis dominum Gualam diaconum cardinalem, inter cardinales in iure ciuili peritissimum"; *The Letters and Charters of Cardinal Guala Bicchieri, Papal Legate in England 1216-1218*, ed. by Nicholas Vincent, Woodbridge, Boydell and Brewer, 1996, pp. xli-lxxxviii.

46. Thomas Rymer, *Foedera, Conventiones, Literae et cujuscunque generis Acta Publica inter Reges Angliae et alios…*, London, George Eyre and Andrew Strachan, 1704-1735, i.i.145: Vincent, *Letters and Charters*, pp. 28-29.

47. Heinrich Weber, *Über das Verhältniss Englands zu Rom während der Zeit der Legation des Cardinal Othos in den Jahren 1237-1241*, Berlin, Weidmannsche Buchhandlung, 1883; Dorothy Williamson, "Some Aspects of the Legation of Cardinal Otto in England, 1237-1241", *English Historical Review*, 64 (1949), pp. 145-173; Bruno Galland, "Les hommes de la culture dans la diplomatie pontificale au XIIIe siècle", *Mélanges de l'École Française de Rome Moyen Age*, 108 (1996), pp. 615-643: 631-632; Pietro Silanos, "Ottone da Tonengo", *Dizionario Biografico degli Italiani*, vol. LXXX, Rome, Istituto della Enciclopedia italiana, 2014, pp. 4-7.

48. *GC Opera*, vol. I, p. 119; Powicke, "Gerald of Wales", p. 124. Gerald may have revised it at a slightly later date: Bartlett, *Gerald of Wales: A Voice of the Middle Ages*, p. 178;

Gervase of Tilbury probably visited Rome in the retinue of an inept emperor. Otto IV, a nephew of King John, had grown up in England and was elected to the imperial crown in October 1209. Of all the accounts we have been considering, *Otia Imperialia* remains in some ways the most puzzling. Is it simply a *divertissement*, or is there a "mirror for princes" lurking within its voluminous pages?[49] There is no evidence that Otto ever read the treatise or even had it read to him.[50] Gervase's aim was to present information that was generally known, but served up in an entertaining way. There is little that is original in the *Otia*, and it was not intended to tax either the emperor's attention span or his intellect. It is clear that, in his descriptions of Rome's monuments, Gervase made extensive use of the *Mirabilia urbis*. But within this mixture of lively stories and marvels, he reveals a new alertness to the natural world. His references to birds have nothing of the ornithological accuracy (or occasional fantasy) of those in the *Topographica hibernica*.[51] He never approaches the delicate precision of Gerald's description of Hugh of Lincoln's tame whooper swan.[52] But Gervase could also be a scientific experimentalist, as is shown by the episode of the flies in the refectory of Notre Dame de l'Espinar at Barjols:[53]

> I am going to tell you something of which I have personal experience. In the kingdom of Arles, in the province of Aix there is a small town called Barjols, in which there is a notable collegiate foundation of venerable age; it is lavishly endowed with estates, and excites the envy of neighbouring churches by its lavish hospitality. It has a refectory, built long ago, in which no fly can be made to stay. I had learned of this strange matter by

John J. Hagen, *The Jewel of the Church*: *A Translation of* Gemma ecclesiastica *by Giraldus Cambrensis*, Leiden, Brill, 1979, p. xvi.

49. Gervase of Tilbury, *Otia Imperialia*, pp. xli-xliii.

50. *Ibid.*, pp. 558-559.

51. Urban Holmes, "Gerald the Naturalist", *Speculum*, 11 (1936), pp. 110-1121; Antonia Gransden, "Realistic Observation in Twelfth-Century England", *Speculum*, 47 (1972), pp. 29-51; Brunsdon Yapp, *Birds in Medieval Manuscripts*, London, The British Library, 1981, pp. 49, 118; Wilma George, Brunsdon Yapp, *The Naming of the Beasts*, London, Duckworth, 1991, pp. 168-169.

52. *GC Opera*, vol. VII, p. 74: "Erat enim tanto fere cigno robustior, quanto cignus ansere major; cigno tamen in omnibus et praecipue in olore et candour simillimus. Praeter quantitatem etiam hoc distante, quod tumorem in rostro atque negredinem more cignorum non praeferebat; quinimmo locum eundem rostri plenum, croceosque decenter colore, una cum capite ut colli parte superior distinctum habebat". A first recension is datable c. 1198. The black bill with yellow wedge sides is accurately distinguished in shape and colour from the orange and black bill of the mute swan: Nicholas Hammond, Michael Everett, *Birds of Britain and Europe*, London, Pan Books, 1980, pp. 51-52.

53. Gervase of Tilbury, *Otia Imperialia*, pp. 574, 575: "Rem expertam loquar. Est in regno Arelatensi, provincia Aquensi vicus Bariolis nomine, in quo canonica singularis fundata est antiquitate veneranda, possessionibus honorifice fundata [...] hospitalitate vicinis ecclesiis invidiosa. In hac est refectorium, ab antiquo edificatum, in quo nulla musca detineri potest. Huis rei novitatem mihi per auditum cognitam ad probationem per experimentum ducturus, accessi sedulus explorator si quo melis uel cuiusuis pinguedinis linimento scutellis musce, ut assolent, insiderent. Profecto rem rumore comperiens veriorem, volens fallacium ingeniosam cogitationis humane frustratam quadam violentia adiuvare, muscarum venator effectus, predam in refectorio melli, lacti, ad pinguedini supersterno. Tunc maior excrevit admiratio, cum vim animi et violentiam corporis a me temptatam perpendo cassari; sicque cum fide facta de auditis stupor est augmentatus".

> hearsay and wanted to test it by an experiment. So I came as an eager investigator to see if flies would settle, as they usually do on platters with a smearing of honey or some other sticky substance on them. I discovered that the matter was in truth more than a rumour. Deciding to adopt violent measures in support of my ingenious ruse, a product of human thinking which had so far failed, I turned into a hunter of flies, and strewed my prey over honey, milk and fat in the refectory. Then my amazement increased, when I observed that the mental energy and physical force which I had invested were in vain. And so while I came to believe what I had heard, my stupefaction was intensified.

This was obviously far less drastic than the experiments on animals and birds by Otto IV's successor, Frederick II of Hohenstaufen, but it is a reflection of the new mindset. Gervase, like Frederick, was also interested in classical cameos, and he thought of the Roman sarcophagi at Les Alyscamps.[54]

Thus, while Gervase, like Gerald and Thomas, were in Rome "on business", Master Gregory's reason for being there is at once more enigmatic and more nebulous. Gregory clearly had time on his hands in Rome. He used his sojourn to extend his knowledge of the classical world and to buttress his reading with direct experience of the monuments themselves.[55] This, of course, was very different from the approach taken by the King's brother, Henri de Blois, Bishop of Winchester. Henri was mockingly skewered by John of Salisbury's apt quotation from Horace while he was in Rome between 1149 and 1151, insatiably collecting classical statues to take home to Winchester.[56] He was perhaps assuaging his disappointment after his scheme for raising his bishopric to an archdiocese was blocked by Pope Eugenius III. It may nevertheless be the case that his Roman acquisitions had an impact on the sculptors of his cathedral.[57]

54. Gervase gives the etymology of *capmahu* (= camaieu/cameo): *ibid.*, p. 614. I have not seen Falk Quenstedt, Thilo Renz, "Kritik und Konstruktion der Wunderbaren in der Otia Imperialia des Gervasius von Tilbury", in *Das Wunderbaren Dimensionen einer Phänomene in Kunst und Kultur*, ed. by Stefanie Kreuzer and Uwe Durst, Paderborn, Wilhem Fink, 2018, pp. 251-262.

55. It may be that he was making good use of his time in the city while waiting for a legal case to reach trial.

56. John of Salisbury, *The* Historia Pontificalis *of John of Salisbury*, ed. and transl. by Marjorie Chibnall, Oxford, Oxford University Press, 1986, pp. 78-79: "...Henricum Wintoniensem, qui Romam profectus in persona propria satisfecit [...] 79 Cum vero episcopus preter absolutionem se nichil optinere posse videret, accepta licentia rediens veteras statuas emit Rome, quas Wintoniam deferri fecit. Vnde, cum eum vidisset gramaticus quidam barba prolixa et philosophi gravitate ceteris in curia spectabiliorem idola coemere, subtili et laborioso magis quam studioso gentilium fabrefacta, sic lusit in eum: 'Insanit veteres statuas Damasippus emendo' [Horace, Satires, II, iii, 64: "Damasippus is mad in buying old statues"]... 80 Fuit qui suis pro episcopo verbis sed illius fortasse spiritu responderet, ipsum hac industria Romanis subtraxisse deos suos ne possent (ad quod proni videbantur) eis veteres cerimonias exhibere qui iam per innatam et inolitam et radicatam avariciam spiritualiter idolis serviebant" ["...engaged in buying up idols, carefully made by the heathen in the error of their hands rather than their minds"]. Michael Camille, *The Gothic Idol: Ideology and Image-Making in Medieval Art*, Cambridge, Cambridge University Press, 1989, p. 80: "inborn, inveterate and ineradicable avarice already made them idol-worshippers in spirit". Luchterhand, "*Mirabilia* - Die Antiken Roms", pp. 90-92.

57. Paul Williamson, *Gothic Sculpture 1140-1300*, London/New Haven, Yale University Press, 1995, p. 113. The sculptor of the surviving statue perhaps an *Ecclesia* of c. 1230 at Winchester shows a striking familiarity with the antique. Heinz Roosen-Runge, "Ein Werke

We can exclude with some certainty that Master Gregory was there for self-improvement. He did not engage in conversations with cardinals during casual encounters. However, one fundamental aspect of the text needs to be confronted. It has recently been suggested that Gregory may not have visited Rome, and that his information was culled from known sources or simply invented for parodical effect.[58] This theory can be categorically rejected. Many arguments speak against it. First of all, the context in which the manuscript was found suggests that it was taken seriously; in the early 14th century, the chronicler Ranulph Higden (1280-1364) considered it a reliable source and paraphrased it in his *Polychronicon*.[59] The *Narracio* lacks both the deliberate Latin howlers, which begged for correction, and the sly misinformation that characterises *Jacobus*, the so-called *Codex Calixtinus*.[60] That text has plausibly been identified as the working manual of a nomadic grammar master that was intended to teach boys Latin and music. On the contrary, the *Narracio* is well written and shows a familiarity with the *cursus*, the rhythmical prose used in high ecclesiastical circles. The use of rhetorical figures is measured and generally unobtrusive. Its interest in antique statuary has the ring of authenticity, as we shall see. It admittedly owes a considerable amount to the *Mirabilia urbis Romae*, but that dependence has rarely been doubted. It has been authoritatively demonstrated that the *Mirabilia* is not a "papal" text, as was recently claimed, but a product of renascent republican circles in Rome during the 1140s.[61] The assertion that Gregory's descriptions are greatly exaggerated for comic effect is to seriously overstate the case. The intended purpose of Gregory's *Narracio* was certainly to be an enjoyable read, but it is emphatically not a spoof.[62]

englischer Grossplastik des 13. Jahrhunderts and die Antike", in *Festschrift Hans R Hahnloser zum 60. Geburtstag 1959*, ed. by Ellen Beer and Paul Hofer, Basle, Birkhäuser, 1961, pp. 103-112.

58. William Kynan-Wilson, "Subverting the Message: Master Gregory's Reception of and Response to the *Mirabilia Urbis Romae*", *Journal of Medieval History*, 44/3 (2018), pp. 347-364. Some of its descriptions, it has been suggested, were composed tongue in cheek; Paul Binski, *Gothic Wonder*, London/New Haven, Yale University Press, 2014, p. 29.

59. Montague Rhodes James, *A Descriptive Catalogue of the Manuscripts in the Library of St. Catherine's College, Cambridge*, Cambridge, Cambridge University Press, 1925, pp. 10-12; *Master Gregorius: The Marvels of Rome*, ed. by Osborne, p. 1. Taylor, *The "Universal Chronicle" of Ranulph Higden*, pp. 54, 81.

60. Christopher Hohler, "A Note on Jacobus", *Journal of the Warburg and Courtauld Institutes*, 35 (1972), pp. 31-80: 31. The author himself called his book *Jacobus*: "Ex re signatur / Jacobus liber iste vocatur / ipsum scribenti / sit gloria sitque legenti"; *ibid.*, pp. 31, 34. "Jacobus was not compiled purely to entertain: the musical instruction is entirely serious": Alison Stones, "Le culte de Saint Jacques entre Compostelle et Pistoia et le rôle du chanoine Rainerius", in *Pèlerinages, origines, succès et avenir*, ed. by Térence Le Deschaut de Monredon, Cahors, Éditions patrimoniales de la ville de Cahors, 2019, pp. 39-48.

61. Ingo Herklotz, "Der Campus Lateranensis im Mittelalter", *Römisches Jahrbuch*, 22 (1985), pp. 1-43: 26-28; Ingo Herklotz, *Gli eredi di Costantino. Il papato, il Laterano e la propaganda visive nel XII secolo*, Rome, Viella, 2000, pp. 66-70; Dario Internullo, "'Decus Urbis'. Un'altra prospettiva sui Mirabilia di Roma e le origini del decoro urbano (secoli XII-XV)", *Quaderni Storici*, 1 (2020), pp. 159-183.

62. I have benefited from discussions on this point with Ingo Herklotz, Mary Carruthers and John Osborne.

4. The Visitors' Rome

In the medieval European imagination, the first glimpse of Rome to greet cultivated visitors was to an extent conditioned by Hildebert of Lavardin's great poem "*Par tibi Roma*".[1] Master Gregory provides a more prosaic, but nonetheless artful, prologue:

> I strongly recommend the wonderful panorama of the whole city. There is so great a forest of towers, and so many palatial buildings, that no one has counted them. When I saw it for the first time, at a distance from the slope of the hill (the Monte Mario), after I had spent some time admiring this stunningly picturesque sight, I thanked God, mighty throughout the entire world, who had here rendered the works of man wondrously and indescribably beautiful. For although all of Rome lies in ruins, nothing intact can be compared to this.

For both poet and pragmatist, it was clear that Rome was incomparable. Gregory cited Hildebert's poem, probably from memory, but in a very perceptive reading, picking up its deep borrowings from Lucan. Implicit, indeed, is Gregory's knowledge of Hildebert's second poem on Rome, which saw the towering magnificence of its ruins as a prelude to its present and future existence as the capital of Christianity, although this is not a view to which our insular traveller subscribed emphatically (Fig. 5).[2]

The horizon of Rome provided an uncompromisingly secular prologue to Master Gregory's first glimpse of Rome.[3] It was clearly an exceptional viewpoint. Earlier, Gerald had viewed the Eternal City primarily as the shrine of great martyrs and the churches built in their memory. Prior to Constantine's foundation of the Lateran, the faith had been practiced in secrecy. For him, Rome had been

1. Texts are in *Hildeberti Cenomannensis episcopi carmina minora*, ed. by Brian A. Scott, Leipzig, Teubner, 1969, pp. 22-24.

2. Bruce Gibson, "Hildebert of Lavardin on the Monuments of Rome", in *Word and Context in Latin Poetry: Studies in Memory of David West*, ed. by Anthony Woodman and Jaap Wisse, Cambridge, Cambridge University Press, 2017, pp. 131-154; *Master Gregorius: The Marvels of Rome*, ed. by Osborne, p. 18, n. 4; Luchterhand, "*Mirabilia* - Die Antiken Roms", p. 91. A late 15th-century view from the Monte Mario is in the *Codex Escurialensis* fol. 7v; Hermann Egger, *Römische Veduten*, vol. II, Vienna, Anton Schroll, 1931, plate 102.

3. While Kynan-Wilson, "Subverting the Message", p. 348 points out that the enumeration of towers and gates had already occurred earlier in the *Mirabilia*, this does not prove that Gregory's prologue was merely imitative. See p. 61 below.

characterised by the five great churches: the Lateran, Saint Peter's, the abbey of San Paolo *fuori le mura*, the abbey of San Lorenzo *fuori le mura* and, finally, Santa Maria Maggiore. They each had differing governance, regular or monastic. He was precise regarding the Lateran dedication: it was first to the Saviour, secondarily to the Baptist and finally to St John the Evangelist.[4] Its pre-eminence was indisputable, although it was consistently undermined by the discontent of the clergy at Saint Peter's. He gracefully offered an opposing, consolatory argument to the Vatican: because of Christ's charge to Peter, "Quare videtur ejus basilica caeterarum omnium esse non immerito fundamentum" ("Wherefore his basilica not undeservedly seems to be the basis of all others").[5]

Not every contemporary was as enraptured on arrival as Master Gregory. What, in reality, confronted the British visitor when one reached the Eternal City? A letter from an unknown English pen describes the Roman situation starkly, in a vitriolic characterisation with echoes of Cicero's denunciation of Catiline:

> But if you may have safety, yet the general affliction will not be concealed, since, so it is said, you have to be slaves under the sway of summer heat. There is a persistent and unbearable boiling heat there, stinking waters, coarse food, clammy air, clouds of flies, countless scorpions, a filthy people, abhorrent, untrustworthy and quarrelsome, and the city within its entire circumference abounds in caves, and the caverns are full of poisonous reptiles, from which exhale an infected and infectious smoke; thus, all who then dwell there generally die, so that, of thousands, scarcely ten escape. Those therefore whom it has belched forth in the wrath of the sea, greedy Rome will devour in a poisonous quagmire.[6]

A more or less contemporaneous account of the appalling situation in the Septizonium, where the cardinals were confined, by an anti-papal Senator, Matteo

4. *GC Opera*, vol. IV, ch. 1, p. 270. This is perhaps to be expected from an observer who, in *De iure et statu Menevensis Ecclesiae*, had already composed a treatise on the status of cathedrals. See Eivor Andersen Oftestad, *The Lateran Church in Rome and the Ark of the Covenant: Housing the Holy Relics of Jerusalem*, Cambridge, Cambridge University Press, 2019, pp. 144-146.

5. *GC Opera*, vol. IV, ch. 1, p. 271.

6. Translation by Leofranc Holford-Strevens. "Quod si securitas vobis esse potuerit generalis tamen afflictio non latebit, quia cum sub estivi caloris dominio vos servos oporteat ibi esse sic dicitur ibi perseverans et intolerabilis caloris ebullitio, acquarum putrefactio, ciborum grossities, aer palpabilis, muscarum habundantia et copia scorpionum, gens immunda, gens abominabilis, gens pessima, gens furoris fitque ibi civitas infra totam circumferentiam cavernosa caverneque plene reptilibus venenosis ex quibus fumus infectus et inficiens evaporat, sic omnes ibi tunc morantes generaliter moriuntur quod de millibus decem vix evadere possunt. Sic ergo quos indignatio maris evomuerit, vorax Roma venenosa voragine devorabit. Sic ergo quos indignatio maris evomuerit, vorax Roma venenosa voragine devorabit; et qui Scillam evasisse crediderit, incit in Caribdim". Jean-Louis A. Huillard-Breholles, *Historia Diplomatica Friderici Secundi sive constitutiones, privilegia, mandata, instrumenta quae supersunt istius imperatoris et filiorum ejus. Accedunt epistolae paparum et documenta varia*, vol. II, Paris, Henri Plon, 1859, pp. 1077-1085: 1081. See also Cicero, *Oratio in Catilinam, I-IV*, transl. by Coll Macdonald, Cambridge, MA, Harvard University Press, 1977, pp. 69-70. The mention of caverns is intriguing. Does it refer to either Roman ruins, or perhaps catacombs, that were then accessible? For the latter, see Julian Gardner, *Roman Crucible: The Artistic Patronage of the Papacy 1198-1304*, Munich, Hirmer Verlag, 2013, p. 223.

Orsini, to hasten the election of a new pope, fully confirms these horrors (Fig. 6).[7] The English cardinal Robert of Somercotes did not survive this harrowing experience, and his austere tomb epitaph is still to be seen in the church of San Crisogono.[8]

All this suggests that a visit to Rome was not without its hazards. The witnesses we are considering had a business-like attitude to Rome. They were there for important reasons of their own. Thus, the churches they mention are limited to the great basilicas, where they probably collected indulgences, and important buildings connected with their missions, in particular the Lateran Palace.[9] Those more fortunate might visit Rome during a papal election. The subsequent celebrations could be extensive, as the *Liber censuum* attests.[10] Processions, crowds and trumpets would accompany the papal coronation. Yet it

7. Karl Hampe, "Ein ungedruckter Bericht über das Konklave von 1241 im römischen Septizonium", *Sitzungsberichte der Heidelberger Akademie der Wissenschaften Philosophisch-historische Klasse*, 4 (1913), pp. 1-34: 26-31. On 19 November 1241 the cardinals, from the safety of Anagni, reported the terrifying conditions of the papal conclave: "Numquid semivivos, qui adhuc portant stigmata tormentorum…"; "…super testitudines nostri capitibus imminentes / 29 a custodibus decubantibus in eisdem urina sepius fundebatur, que per rimas et crepitudines super unius fratris notri cubiculum, velud olens locium et de altera, ubi sua purgamenta sternebant, mixta imbribus super alterum noctibus defluebat…"; "Nonne venerabilis alter frater [prob. Somercotes] delatus violenter est in secreto mortuorum, super quem spuebant et lamentationum funebrium in fausta carmina derisorie decantabant et percuciebant durius sub grabato cum arcubus balistarum? […] 30 Nec est aliquatenus obmittendum, quod senator nos concuciebat terroribus et tonitruis […] protinus mitratum papam de monstraremus, alioquin effossum pape cadaver in medio nostrum poneret, ut intollerabilis corruptela fetoris et confusionis et doloris immensitas absque mora fratres extingeueret semivivos". The use of the rare term *stigmata* (p. 28) is noteworthy at this date.

8. Cardinal-deacon of Sant'Eustachio (1238-1241) and *auditor litterarum contradictarum*: see Paravicini-Bagliani, *Cardinali di Curia*, pp. 130-137; Jane Sayers, "Robert of Somercotes", in *Dictionary of National Biography*, vol. LI, p. 862. For the tomb slab, see Jörg Garms et al., *Die mittelalterlichen Grabmäler in Rom und Latium von 13. bis 15. Jahr-hundert. I. Die Grabplatten und Tafeln*, Rome/Vienna, Verlag der Österreichischen Akademie der Wissenschaften, 1981 (Publikationen de Österreichischen Kultur-instituts in Rom, II, Abteilung, Quellen 5. Reihe I), X. S. Crisogono, N. 1, pp. 69-70, reproduced as Tab. 208. The epitaph reads (H)IC·Q(VI)ESCIT·IN·D(OMI)NO·ROB(ER)TVS·GRATE·MEMORIE·S(AN)C(T)I·EVSTACHII·/DIACONVS·CARDINALIS·NATIONE·ANGLIC(VS)·Q(VI)·OBIIT·VI·KAL(ENDAS)·OCTOB(RIS)·/ANNO·D(OMI)NICE·INCARNATIONIS·Mo·CCo·QVADRAGESIMO·PRIMO.For medieval Roman epitaphs, see Iiro Kajanto, *Classical and Christian Studies in the Latin Epitaphs of Medieval and Renaissance Rome*, Helsinki, Suomalainen Tiedeakatemia, 1980 remains basic. See, more recently, Marco Guardo, "Epitafi di Papi Cardinali ed altri dignitari della Curia Pontificia tematiche e stile nell'epigrafia poetica del XIII secolo", *Archivio della Società Romana di Storia Patria*, 122 (1999), pp. 125-134; and Marco Guardo, *Titulus e tumulus*, Rome, Viella, 2008.

9. There is a very thought-provoking, but ultimately unsatisfactory, attempt to evoke the contemporary experience of the physical environment of the papal palace by Fonnesberg-Schmidt, Kynan Wilson, "Smiling, Laughing, and Joking at Rome", pp. 153-181.

10. *Le Liber Censuum de l'Église Romaine*, vol. II, ed. by Paul Fabre and Louis Duchesne, Paris, Fontemoing et Cie., 1910, p. 19; Susan Twyman, *Papal Ceremonial at Rome in the Twelfth Century*, Martlesham, Boydell Press, 2010; Julian Gardner, "The Cardinals'

was an event that none of our visitors appear to have experienced. Sight-seeing was at a minimum for most, although here Gregory is an exception once again; he looked around for himself, and what he wanted to see was the testimony of the classical past. Additionally, we should bear in mind that, almost inevitably but often unwittingly, we are looking at the panorama of early 13th-century Rome through the medium of drawings and prints made several centuries later.

The great churches of Rome were linked not only by papal privilege, the stational liturgy, but also by rivalry and dispute: Gerald was expert in both. He accurately described the rancorous relationship between the chapters of the cathedral of Rome St John Lateran and the Vatican burial site of the Prince of the Apostles.[11] Yet his is the most extensive and accurate description of the status of the individual basilicas of all our authors. A great deal of what Gervase says is taken directly from the old urban guide-books.

Gregory had no time for churches. For him, they are mere signifiers with which to locate classical monuments and statues. The main centres of western Christendom, St John in the Lateran and St Peter's, get only the most cursory reference, and the Pantheon, which fascinated him, is examined as a Roman building rather than as the medieval church of Santa Maria Rotonda.

What was happening to the great early Christian basilicas between 1198 and 1240, which our visitors are likely to have experienced? In the churches, they all mention that major decorative works were under way.

But the Campus Lateranensis, the space in front of the cathedral of Rome and to the north of it, was also freighted with meaning (Fig. 7).[12] It was there that the Romans assembled to acclaim a new pope and on other ceremonial occasions. There, in front of the portico of the refurbished papal palace, the ancient bronzes that caught Gregory's restless eye were also gathered, perhaps by Pope Zacharias (741-742).[13] These included the wolf, the so-called Colossus (a gigantic bronze

Music: Musical Interests at the Papal Curia c. 1200 – c. 1304", *Early Music History*, 34 (2015), pp. 97-132.

11. *GC Opera*, vol. IV, bk IV, ch. II, p. 270: "…quamvis tamen altercationibus variis et assertionibus, probabilibus quidem et verisimilibus, clerus ecclesiae sancti Petri constanter obloqui videatur et oblatrare, suam praeponere basilicam moliendo modis omnibus et enitendo". For a recent summary of this rivalry, see Carola Jäggi, "Mater et Caput Omnium Ecclesiarum: Visual Strategies in the Rivalry between San Giovanni in Laterano and San Pietro in Vaticano", in *The Basilica of Saint John Lateran to 1600*, ed. by Lex Bosman, Ian Haynes and Paolo Liverani, Cambridge, Cambridge University Press, 2020, pp. 294-317.

12. Herklotz, "Der Campus Lateranensis im Mittelalter", *passim*; Ingo Herklotz, "Der mittelalterliche Fassadenportikus der Lateranbasilika und seine Mosaiken, Kunst und Propaganda am Ende des 12. Jahrhunderts", *Römisches Jahrbuch der Bibliotheca Hertziana*, 25 (1989), pp. 25-95; Herklotz, *Gli eredi*, pp. 41-88; Chris Wickham, *Medieval Rome*, Oxford, Oxford University Press, 2015, pp. 335-337.

13. John Osborne, *Rome in the Eighth Century*, Cambridge, Cambridge University Press, 2020, pp. 148, 157; *Magister Gregorius*, ed. by Huygens, p. 30. Herklotz, "Der Campus Lateranensis im Mittelalter", p. 18 and n. 83. For the *Lupa* and its early medieval origin, see Cécile Dulière, *Lupa romana. Études de philologie, d'archéologie et d'histoire anciennes*, 17, Rome, Institut Historique Belge de Rome, 1979, vol. I, 23 ff.; *Master Gregorius*, ed. by Osborne, pp. 96-97; Herklotz, *Gli eredi*, pp. 57-61, 217.

head of an unidentified Roman emperor), and the other bronze fragments now in the Capitoline Museums.[14] By this period, there was also the bronze inscription of the Emperor Vespasian, the *Lex de imperio*, which Gregory tried and failed to read.[15] Gregory provides the first certain reference to the presence of the *Lupa*, although he scoffs at its identification as the she-wolf that suckled Romulus and Remus (Fig. 8).[16] Nevertheless, his account rings true as the observation of an eyewitness:

> In the portico of the winter palace of the lord pope are a bronze statue of the she-wolf, which is supposed to have suckled Romulus and Remus [...] the bronze wolf stalks a bronze ram, which also stands in front of the palace, and from its mouth water pours for washing one's hands. Water for hand-washing used to run from the wolf's teats, but now its feet are broken and it has been removed from its original place.[17]

The bronze ram, which was apparently placed close to the wolf, has now vanished (Fig. 9).[18] Gregory identified the gigantic imperial bronze head in the same location as a fragment from the Colossus of Nero, which occupied a vestibule of the *Domus Aurea* (Fig. 10). He attributed its destruction to Pope Gregory the Great, who had gained a reputation in the Middle Ages as the destroyer of pagan statues.[19] The pope was plainly the English visitor's *bête noire*. Yet, Gregory's

14. Osborne, *Rome in the Eighth Century*, pp. 148-158; Wickham, *Medieval Rome*, pp. 335-336; Anna M. Carruba, *La lupa capitolina*, Rome, Bretschneider, 2006. Gilda Bartoloni, *La lupa capitolina. Nuove prospettive di studio*, Rome, Bretschneider, 2010; Herklotz, "Der Campus Lateranensis im Mittelalter", p. 22. A medieval date has been posited for the wolf. It seems, on balance, preferrable to accept the traditional view that it is of Etruscan origin. I am grateful to John Osborne for sharing an unpublished lecture on this subject with me. Francis Haskell, Nicholas Penny, *Taste and the Antique: The Lure of Classical Sculpture 1500-1900*, New Haven/London, Yale University Press, 1981, pp. 335-337.

15. Herklotz, "Der Campus Lateranensis im Mittelalter", p. 21 and p. 22, fig. 6: "Ante hanc enea tabula est, ubi pociora legis precepta scripta sunt [...] In hac tabula plura legi set pauca intellexi". Nardella, *Il fascino*, p. 172; Osborne, *Rome in the Eighth Century*, p. 153.

16. *Master Gregorius*, ed. by Osborne, p. 96: "imago enea illius lupe, que dicitur Remum et Romulum aduisse. Sed hoc quidem fabulosam est". The aetiology he then provides, that Lupa was "*quedam mulier eximie pulchritudinis antiquitus Romae fuit*", is considerably more unbelievable. Nardella, *Il fascino*, p. 172.

17. *Master Gregorius*, ed. by Osborne, p. 36: "In porticu etiam ante palatium hiemale palatium domini pape est imago enea illius lupe, que dicitur Remum et Romulum aluisse [...] Hec autem lupa enea arieti eneo insidiatur, qui ante palatium prefatum aquam abluendis manibus ore remittit. Lupa etiam quondam singulis mammis aquam abluendis minabus emittebat, set nunc fractis pedibus a loco suo divulsa est". Nardella, *Il fascino*, p. 172.

18. Nardella, *Il fascino*, p. 172. An ancient bronze of a ram, now in the Museo Archeologico of Palermo, may provide an impression of this lost statue. Originally one of a pair, it was placed above the entry door of Castello Maniace, the Hohenstaufen fortress at Syracuse. See Henning Gans, "Der Widder von Kastell Maniace. Eine Bronze atoninischer Zeit?" *Antike Kunst*, 48 (2005), pp. 73-99.

19. "Hanc autem statuam post destructionem omnium statuarum que Romam fuerunt et deturpacionem beatus Gregorius [...] destruxit", Nardella, *Il fascino*, p. 152. Osborne, *Rome in the Eighth Century*, pp. 152-153; Tilman Buddensieg, "Gregory the Great, Destroyer of Pagan Idols: The History of a Medieval Legend Concerning the Decline of Ancient Art and Literature", *Journal of the Warburg and Courtauld Institutes*, 28 (1965), pp. 44-65. Luchterhand, "*Mirabilia* – Die Antiken Roms", p. 93.

appreciation of its technical finesse is another remarkable example of his aesthetic judgement: "Although of dreadful size, one can nonetheless admire in them the great skill of their maker, and indeed nothing of the perfect beauty of the human head or hand is lacking in any part. It is quite astonishing how the fluid craftsmanship can simulate soft hairs in solid bronze, and if you look intently, transfixed by its splendour, it gives the appearance of being about to move and speak".[20] This *ekphraseis* compares well with that of the marble Venus he so admired. These bronzes, and above all the celebrated equestrian statue, made the site a magnet for all cultivated visitors.

The new colonnaded portico of the Lateran basilica itself, signed by the prominent architect Niccolo Angeli, was of recent construction, most probably in the last two decades of the 12th century.[21] Its architrave was originally decorated with a series of small mosaic scenes of the Legend of Silvester and Constantine, with a representation of the Donation prominent.[22] A chapel dedicated to St Thomas occupied part of this structure. For Gregory, it may have in part been the judicial functions of the new Lateran portico that mattered. Certainly, there is early evidence in northern Europe that church façade precincts acted as places of justice.[23] Set in the distant "*disabitato*", just within the city walls, it was still

20. *Master Gregorius*, ed. by Osborne, p. 23: "Nam cum horrende magnitudinis sint, mira tamen laus artificis in his appariet. Nichil quippe habet perfecte pulchritudinis humanum capud vel manus, quod his ulla partis desit: miro enim modo ars fusilis in ere rigido molles mentitur capillos. Quod siquis defixis luminibus attencius inspexerti, moturo et locoturo simillimum videtur: nullum namque signum ut aiunt, tanta cura vel impensis in urbe conditum fuit". Nardella, *Il fascino*, p. 152.

21. NICOLAVS ANGELI FECIT HOC OPVS. On the portico, see Ingo Herklotz, "Der mittelalterliche Fassadenportikus der Lateranbasilika und seine Mosaiken, Kunst und Propaganda am Ende des 12. Jahrhunderts", *Römisches Jahrbuch der Bibliotheca Hertziana*, 25 (1989), pp. 25-95; Herklotz, *Gli eredi*, pp. 161, 218. Peter Cornelius Claussen, Daniela Mondini, Darko Senekovic, *Die Kirchen der Stadt Rom im Mittelalter 1050-1300*, Bd. 3 G-L, Stuttgart, Franz Steiner Verlag, 2010 (Corpus Cosmatorum, II/3), pp. 63-88: 77. Claussen, p. 89 now agrees with a late 12th-century date. Lex Bosman, "Constantine's Spolia: A Set of Columns for San Giovanni in Laterano and the Arch of Constantine in Rome", in *The Basilica of St. John Lateran*, p. 183. Fragments of the portico have recently been identified: *Il portico medievale di San Giovanni in Laterano: I frammenti ritrovati*, ed. by Anna Maria De Strobel, Città del Vaticano, Edizioni Musei Vaticani, 2019.

22. Herklotz, *Gli eredi*, pp. 166-169. Claussen, Mondini, Senekovic, *Die Kirchen der Stadt Rom*, pp. 79-84; Serena Romano, ed., *Il Duecento e la cultura gotica 1198 – 1287 ca.*, Milan, Jaca Book, 2012, pp. 372 ff.

23. Herklotz, "Der Campus Lateranensis im Mittelalter", p. 21. Julian Gardner, "Thirteenth-Century Gothic Façades in Italy", in *Medioevo: arte e storia, Atti del Convegno internazionale di studi, Parma 18- 22 settembre 2007*, ed. by Arturo Carlo Quintavalle, Milan, 2008, pp. 669-680: 669 and 578, n. 20; Peter Wiek, "Das Strassburger Münster Untersuchungen über die Mitwirkung des Stadtbürgertums am Bau bischöflicher Kathedralkirchen im Spätmittelalter", *Zeitschrift für die Geschichte des Oberrheins*, 107 (1959), pp. 40-113; Peter Cornelius Claussen, *Chartres-Studien Zu Vorgeschichte, Funktion und Skulptur der Vorhallen*, Wiesbaden, Franz Steiner Verlag, 1975; Barbara Deimling, "Das mittelalterliche Kirchenportal in seiner rechtsgeschichtliche Bedeutung", in *Romanik*, ed. by Rolf Toman, Cologne, Feierabend, 1996, pp. 324-327. For Rome, see Herklotz, "Der Campus Lateranensis im Mittelalter", p. 20.

a religious and political centre, and, unlike the precincts of the Vatican, it was a space shared between the papacy and the citizens.[24]

Given their connections and the purpose of their visits, they may well have seen the great political murals and the Oratorio di San Nicola in the Lateran palace, also commissioned by its builder Calixtus II (1119-1124) and decorated by his successors. These ostentatiously celebrated the victory of the reform papacy in the investiture controversy (Fig. 11).[25] They are mentioned by John of Salisbury and must have impressed all the litigants and petitioners who saw them. In John's words: "Thus to the glory of the Fathers, as the Lateran palace bears witness, wherein even the laity read this truth made visible in pictures – to the glory of the Fathers, I say, all schismatics thrust upon the Church by the power of this world, are given to the pontiffs to be their footstool, and posterity records their overthrow as records of her triumph".[26]

Within the oratory itself, in an upper register, appeared the Enthroned Virgin accompanied by angels, with the popes Calixtus II and Anacletus IV kneeling at her feet. Saint Silvester I (314-335) and Saint Anacletus I (976-988) stood at the sides.[27] In a lower zone, flanking a central niche where the titular of the oratory Nicholas of Bari himself stood, were eight standing popes: Gelasius II, Paschal I, Celestine I, Leo I on the left of the niche, and Gregory VII, Alexander II, Gregory I and Anacletus II on the right. The painting is commonly interpreted as a monument to the victorious reformist papacy, and a statement of the essential sanctity of the papal office.[28] Within this context, the Virgin above has also been

24. Krautheimer, *Rome*, pp. 311-317; Wickham, *Medieval Rome*, p. 337.

25. Ingo Herklotz, "Die Beratungsräume Calixtus' II im Lateranpalast und ihre Fresken. Kunst und Propaganda am Ende des Investiturstreits", *Zeitschrift für Kunstgeschichte*, 52 (1989), pp. 145-214. Herklotz, *Gli eredi*; Serena Romano, *Riforma e tradizione 1050-1198. La pittura medievale a Roma*, Milan, Jaca Book, 2006, pp. 270-277.

26. *The Letters of John of Salisbury*, vol. I, *The Early Letters (1153-1161)*, ed. by William J. Millor, Harold E. Butler and Christopher N. L. Brooke, Oxford, Oxford University Press, 1986, no. 124 to Master Ralph of Sarre, pp. 204-207: "Eram enim Romae [1152]… 207 Sic ad gloriam / 208 patrum, teste Laterani palatio, ubi hoc in visibilibus picturis et laici legunt, ad gloriam partum scismatici quos secularis potestas intrusit dantur pontificibus pro scabello, et eorum memoriam recolunt posteri pro triumpho"; Herklotz, "Die Beratungsräume", pp. 152-153.

27. Sant'Anacletus was subsequently altered to Anastasius, when Anacletus came to be considered an anti-pope. See *The Paper Museum of Cassiano del Pozzo, Series A Antiquities and Architecture II. Early Christian and Medieval Antiquities I Mosaics and Wall Paintings from Roman Churches*, ed. by John Osborne and Amanda Claridge, London, Harvey Miller, 1996, no. 22, p. 110. The identification of the original popes was made by Louis Duchesne, "Le nom d'Anaclet II au palais de Latran", *Mélanges d'Archéologie et d'Histoire*, 9 (1889), pp. 355-362. Herklotz, "Die Beratungsräume", pp. 212-214; Romano, *Riforma e Tradizione*, pp. 290-293; Oratorio S. Nicola, Portico Mosaics, pp. 372-374. The murals were destroyed in the 18th century.

28. Christopher Walter, "Papal Political Imagery in the Medieval Lateran Palace", *Cahiers Archéologiques*, 20 (1970), pp. 155-176; Christopher Walter, "Papal Political Imagery in the Medieval Lateran Palace, part 2", *Cahiers Archéologiques*, 21 (1971), pp. 109-136; Ernst Kitzinger, "The Arts as Aspects of a Renaissance Rome and Italy", in *Renaissance and Renewal in the Twelfth Century*, pp. 637-670: 643-645. Herklotz, "Die Beratungsräume", p. 214. But, see now Herklotz, *Gli eredi*, pp. 113-151; Wickham, *Medieval Rome*, pp. 339, 361. On the

interpreted as *Ecclesia*, and its compositional similarities to the venerated icon in Santa Maria in Trastevere are evident.[29] The murals are recorded in coloured drawings by Antonio Eclissi at Windsor Castle and by an engraving probably based on the Eclissi copies.[30] The fact that both kneeling popes have square haloes indicates that they are contemporary pontiffs and suggests that the commission was initiated by Calixtus II and completed by Anacletus II (1130-1138). The sketches are extremely summary, but some suggestive analogies can nevertheless be drawn with murals in the lower church at nearby San Clemente.[31]

It was in this palatial complex that Thomas of Marlborough's case was heard and where Gerald encountered the pope.[32] Gerald, characteristically, claimed intimate access to the pope, and so he may personally have seen the oratory decoration. One might well assume that under Innocent III the political frescoes were also shown to Otto IV and his courtiers in order to emphasise the pre-eminence of the *vicarius Christi*.

He begins his account with the Lateran as first among the principal five churches of Rome. It has regular canons under a prior, whereas the Vatican has canons with a cardinal as archpriest. San Paolo is now a Cluniac monastery. Then follows Santa Maria Maggiore, and San Lorenzo *fuori le mura*, which has monks of the same congregation as at San Paolo, but with separate and distinctive prerogatives. Pre-eminent, despite the dissatisfaction of the Vatican canons, is the Lateran, the basilica of the Saviour with dedications to Saint John the Baptist and Saint John the Evangelist. Through this dedication, the Lateran was truly "caput et vertex omnium ecclesiarum".[33] At the end of the 13th century, this dedication was illustrated in Jacopo Torriti's apse mosaic, the very place where the image of Christ had first manifested itself to the Roman populace.[34] Gerald noted that its New Testament relics surpassed those of the Old Testament.

The apse mosaic in Saint Peter's would most likely have been under construction by 1206, the year of Gerald's pilgrimage and final journey to

concept of *Amtsheiligkeit*, see Ursula Nilgen, "Amtsgenealogie und Amtsheiligkeit: Königs-und Bischofsreihe in der Kunstpropaganda des Hochmittelalters", in *Studien zur mittelalterlichen Kunst 800 – 1250. Festschrift für Florentine Mütherich zum 70. Geburtstag*, ed. by Katharina Bierbrauer, Peter Klein and Willibald Sauerländer, Munich, Prestel Verlag, 1985, pp. 217-234.

29. Ursula Nilgen, "Maria Regina – ein politischer Kultbildtypus", *Römisches Jahrbuch*, 19 (1981), pp. 3-33; Carlo Bertelli, *La Madonna di Santa Maria in Trastevere*, Rome, Eliograf, 1961; Ernst Kitzinger, "A Virgin's Face: Antiquarianism in Twelfth-Century Art", *Art Bulletin*, 62 (1980), pp. 6-19.

30. *The Paper Museum of Cassiano del Pozzo*, pp. 108-117.

31. Herklotz, "Die Beratungsräume", p. 172 and fig. 8; Herklotz, *Gli eredi*, figs 25, 26; Romano, *Riforma e Tradizione*, pp. 270-271 and figs, pp. 135-136.

32. Fonnesberg-Schmidt, Wilson, "Smiling, Laughing, and Joking at Rome", pp. 153-181 take too little account of the visual aspects of the decoration.

33. *GC Opera*, vol. IV, bk IV, p. 272.

34. Gardner, *The Roman Crucible*, p. 257. Honorius III, in a sermon, preached on the feast of the dedication of the basilica spoke of "...Lateranensi basilica, ubi Christus prius [...] publice populo Romano per fidei recogntionem effulsit...". See James M. Powell, "Honorius III's '*Sermo in Dedicatione Ecclesie Lateranensis*' and the Historical-Liturgical Traditions of the Lateran", *Archivum Historiae Pontificiae*, 21 (1983), pp. 195-209.

Rome (Fig. 12).[35] If, as seems very probable, Innocent III also began the apse mosaic at San Paolo *fuori le mura*, which was completed by Venetian mosaicists during the pontificate of Honorius III, the scaffolding would already have been erected in the apse by the same date (Fig. 13).[36] A recently completed apse mosaic was to be seen at Santa Maria Nuova, and a few years earlier, the mosaic of Christ and the Virgin in the apse of Santa Maria in Trastevere had been completed.[37] Both of these would have been visible, and the charisma of Becket and the probable presence of the martyr's favourite icon of the Virgin would have proven irresistibly attractive to an English cleric with time on his hands in Rome.

For Gerald, it was Constantine who built Saint Peter's. Where Saint Peter's is indisputably pre-eminent, not only in Rome but throughout the whole world, is in the number of its lamps, of which 160 burnt daily.[38] In the apse of Saint Peter's, mosaicists, commissioned by Innocent III, were working on an apse mosaic, and had in all probability also begun an apse mosaic at San Paolo. Honorius III was to complete it after Innocent's death by summoning mosaicists from Venice. One of Rome's principal pilgrimage churches thus had an apse mosaic in an up-to-date Byzantine style.[39] None of our insular observers make any allusion to either of these apses. Yet, by the time of Gerald's final visit, work on both must have been under way. Gregory would very likely have seen the cloisters at both San Paolo and the Lateran, yet the new cloisters found no resonance in either his or Gerald's writings. Gerald came to see the relics, while Gregory toured the ancient ruins and their "idols".

Both the great extramural basilicas were Benedictine monasteries and the burial sites of martyrs. San Paolo was Cluniac.[40] Its cloister was added between 1193 and the end of the second decade of the 13th century, initially under the aegis of Cardinal Pietro da Capua, and it was completed by its abbot Giovanni Caetani (Fig. 14).[41] None of our visitors makes any reference to the cloister, although Gervase vividly recounts a meeting with Cardinal Pietro.[42]

35. Romano, *Il Duecento e la cultura gotica*, pp. 62-66, who suggests a starting date of 1205; Gardner, *The Roman Crucible*, pp. 221-222.

36. Romano, *Il Duecento e la cultura gotica*, pp. 77-87; Gardner, *The Roman Crucible*, pp. 222-224.

37. Romano, *Riforma e Tradizione*, pp. 305-311, 335-343; and Lateran Palace fresco Camera Pro Secretis Consiliis, pp. 270-327: 290-293. Oratorio S. Nicola, Portico Mosaics, pp. 372-374.

38. *GC Opera*, vol. IV, bk IV, p. 270. Thomas of Marlborough, on his return from the Fourth Lateran Council, also enhanced the lighting at Evesham abbey: *History of the Abbey of Evesham*, p. 488.

39. Otto Demus, *The Mosaics of San Marco in Venice*, Chicago, Chicago University Press, 1984, vol. II, pp. 19ff; Gardner, *The Roman Crucible*, pp. 219-224. Romano, *Il Duecento e la cultura gotica*, pp. 77-87.

40. Ildefonso Schuster, *La Basilica e il Monastero di S. Paolo fuori le Mura*, Turin, Società Editrice Internazionale, 1934, pp. 43-48.

41. Gustavo Giovannoni, "Opere dei Vassalletti marmorari romani", *L'Arte*, 11 (1908), pp. 262-283: 264-266; Pietro Fedele, "L'iscrizione del Chiostro di San Paolo", *Archivio della R. Società Romana di Storia Patria*, 44 (1921), pp. 269-276; Giovanni B. Giovenale, "Il chiostro medievale di San Paolo fuori le mura", *Bullettino della Commissione Archeologica Comunale di Roma*, 45 (1917), pp. 125-167.

42. See p. 71 below. Thomas of Marlborough also mentions him as reputedly one of the best advocates at the curia: *History of the Abbey of Evesham*, p. 284.

At San Lorenzo *fuori le mura*, major building works were under way at the behest of the papal chancellor Cencius. Somewhat earlier, the double-storeyed cloister at San Lorenzo had been newly built by Clement III (1187-1191) and awkwardly inserted among the existing buildings (Fig. 15).[43] Cencius was to continue to forward this work as cardinal and, later still, as Pope Honorius III (1216-1227).[44] The early Christian church was given a huge western extension with a trabeated nave supported by splendid *spolia* columns. It was the most thorough-going transformation of an early Christian basilica of the 13th century. During his tenure in the chancery, Cencius also remodelled the martyr's shrine and inscribed its fenestella with "[C]ENCIVS HOC FIERI CVM CANCELLARIVS ESSET DE [...]".[45] A portico was added to the façade of the western nave and it, like the Lateran portico before it, was decorated with a mosaic of small narrative episodes. One of these commemorates the crowning of Pierre II de Courtenay, an event that took place in San Lorenzo itself on 9 April 1217, and this probably gives a chronological term of reference for the portico itself. This would agree with the stylistic similarities that have been noted between its architrave and that of the Lateran cloister.[46] Once again, the church gets only the most summary mention from our visitors.

A church that attracted sustained attention from all our visitors was Santa Maria Rotunda, as the Pantheon was known after its re-dedication to the Virgin by Pope Boniface IV early in the 7th century (609). It held a venerated icon of the Virgin, and such icons stood high on the list of visitors and pilgrims to Rome.[47] Gerald carefully described the icon of Christ in the *Sancta sanctorum*, which already stood over the altar.[48] He also repeated, certainly at second hand, the story of the punishment of a Jew who threw a stone at another image of Christ set above the door to the *Sancta sanctorum*. He immediately became mad and died on the spot. The blood was collected and kept as a relic; the wound on the image healed, and the blood dried on the left side of its face but remained visible.[49]

43. *Le Liber Pontificalis: Texte, introduction et commentaire*, ed. by Louis Duchesne, Paris, Ernest Thorin, 1886-1892, vol. II, p. 451: "claustrum apud sanctum Laurentium extra muros ordinavit". Richard Krautheimer, Spencer Corbett, Alfred K. Frazer, *Corpus Basilicarum Christianarum Romae*, Città del Vaticano, Pontificio Istituto di Archeologia Cristiana, 1937-1977 (CBCR), vol. III, p. 13. Joan Barclay Lloyd, "The Architecture of the Medieval Monastery at S. Lorenzo fuori le mura, Rome", in *Architectural Studies in Memory of Richard Krautheimer*, ed. by Cecil L. Striker, Mainz, P. von Zabern, 1996, pp. 99-102.

44. CBCR, vol. II, pp. 139-140.

45. When it was better preserved and was read as "Cencius hic fieri cum cancelarius esset [...] fecit Laurentius et Stephanus suis". See Giuseppe da Bra, *Le iscrizioni latine di S. Lorenzo fuori le mura*, Rome, Scuola Tipografica Pio X, 1931, p. 24.

46. Peter Cornelius Claussen, *Magistri Doctissimi Romani Die romischen Marmorkunstler des Mittelalters*, Stuttgart, Franz Steiner Verlag, 1987, p. 140.

47. Erik Thunø, "The Pantheon in the Middle Ages", in *The Pantheon from Antiquity to the Present*, ed. by Tod Marder and Mark Wilson Jones, Cambridge, Cambridge University Press, 2015, pp. 231-252.

48. See p. 58 below.

49. "Item exemplum de Judaeis qui Romae Lateranense Palatium intrantes, [...] dominicae majestatis depictam imaginem supra ostium quo intratur as sancta sanctorum [...] et imaginem in fronte percussit, statimque sanguis exivit, qui et fluxu largissimo deorsum in

Both Gerald and Gervase commented on the icons they saw both in the Vatican and the Lateran. They discussed them, however, as miracle-working images, rather than making any comment on them as aesthetic objects. This more subjective view was confined to Gregory. The Roman practice of processing icons produced a number of versions of both the *Acheiropoietos* in the *Sancta sanctorum* and of the Virgin.

It is somewhat ironic that Master Gregory, the visitor least interested in churches and church decoration, came to Rome when the great programmes of Innocent III had been completed. His description of the Lateran palace as the "Winter Palace" suggests that the practice of *villeggiatura* had already taken root.[50] But if our visitors were forced to follow the curia to one or other of its summer relocations, they leave little record of it. Gerald delivered his letters to Innocent III at Segni and took his final leave of the pope at Ferentino, both frequent centres of papal summer sojourns in Campagna.[51]

The evident impact of ancient theatre masks and other grotesque heads that appear in the architrave of the Lateran cloister raises questions about the access to and use of ancient sculptural models. Later, we shall examine the enthusiastic reception of Egyptian artefacts in Roman medieval sculpture, but now we must turn to two important surviving examples of ancient sculpture, which uniquely illuminate contemporary attitudes towards ancient sculpture. One of them forms the subject of an important passage in Gregory's *Narracio*. The process by which these ancient artefacts entered the bloodstream of the Cosmati masons can to a very limited extent be documented.

Less well-known than the Capitoline Venus, but in its way more suggestive is the Antinous that today stands in the cortile of the Banca d'Italia (Fig. 16), this 2nd-century sculpture was uncovered during the excavations of 1886 for the foundations of the modern bank building. Rodolfo Lanciani reported the circumstances of its discovery in what he judged to be the remains of a medieval Roman sculptural atelier.[52] The larger-than-life-size statue was found propped

areae pavimentum emanavit". *GC Opera*, vol. II, *Gemma Ecclesiastica*, ed. by John S. Brewer, London, Longman, Green, Longman and Roberts, 1862, p. 103. Hagen, *The Jewel of the Church*, p. 79; Oftestad, *The Lateran Church in Rome*, p. 156.

50. Paravicini Bagliani, "La mobilità della Curia Romana", pp. 170-174. The suggestion was first made by Ingo Herklotz, "Der Campus Lateranensis", p. 19, n. 99.

51. Paravicini Bagliani, "La mobilità della Curia Romana", pp. 162, 228-232; *GC Opera*, vol. III, p. 289.

52. Rodolfo Lanciani, "Delle scoperte avvenute nei disteri pel Palazzo della Banca Nazionale", *Bullettino della Commissione Archeologica Comunale di Roma*, 14 (1886), pp. 184-191: 189, "Il simulacro stavo ritto in piedi con la schiena appogiata alla parete di fondo di una stanza larga appena quattro metri. Il plinto posava, non sul piano antico della stanza ma sopra un strato di rottami". Both arms are lost but the left in origin probably held a spear. It is 228 cm in height. Rodolfo Lanciani, *Storia degli scavi di Roma*, vol. I, Rome, E. Loescher, 1902, p. 10. R.R.R. Smith, *Antinous Boy Made God*, Catalogue of an exhibition at the Ashmolean Museum, Oxford, 28 September 2018 – 24 February 2019, Oxford, 2018, pp. 34-35, 42-43. See the important review by James Davidson, *London Review of Books*, 7 February 2019, p. 19. Lanciani, *Storia degli scavi*, p. 191 tentatively suggested that it came

erect against the rear wall of a small room. It had been damaged by water, and the pitting of the marble is still evident on both legs below the knees. Thus, the figure had clearly been moved from an earlier site to its eventual find-spot, and the legs had been partially scraped to reduce the inequalities in the marble surface. The find-spot evidence strongly suggests that it was being re-utilised, perhaps as a model in a late 12th- or early 13th-century sculptor's atelier.[53] It should be added that this archaeological find strongly supports the contention that the account in Gregory's text of the classical Venus attests to a real event.

Within this context, we should mention the statue of Aesculapius, which was seen by Winckelmann in the Verospi collection he recorded as signed on its socle with "(V)assalectus".[54] It is probable that this figure was to be seen in the context of the statue of Antinous found during the construction of the Banca d'Italia, which was apparently in a Cosmati workshop. Ovid records an important Temple to Aesculapius on the Isola Tiberina.[55] It is plausible that another antique statue was recovered by Vassalectus, who carved his name on the base.[56]

While the statue of a nude Venus might be intensely admired, it was difficult to imitate and place; an ancient *ephebe* might have appeared more adaptable. However, it has not been possible to find any impact of monumental classical statuary in the repertory of the Cosmati workshops. Whilst the cloister architraves at both San Giovanni in Laterano and San Paolo *fuori le mura* reveal the reception of ancient theatre masks and perhaps portrait busts, there is nothing more.[57]

It would therefore seem that the Rome that presented itself to our insular observers passed by them virtually unobserved. Major transformations of the great basilicas, both actualised or under discussion, and which both Gerald and Gervase visited, seem to have passed them by. Only Gregory observed the city as it was, and he was apparently quite uninterested in the great churches.

originally from the Via Nomentana. It is, however, the only statue of Antinous with a firm medieval find-spot. Its closest analogue is the restored figure of Antinous from the Villa Casali, now in the Ny Carlsberg Glyptothek: see Smith, *Antinous*, fig. 15a and p. 31.

53. Despite the loss of both arms and (likely) spear or staff, the statue in in remarkably pure condition when compared to other figures of Antinous. The "bridging" locks of hair covering the ears are still present. Smith, *Antinous*, pp. 22-24. Significantly, the removal of the penis must be medieval. The damage is still visible in old photographs, such as Smith, *Antinous*, fig. 12c. The Bank authorities subsequently added a fig-leaf.

54. "Von der 2. Art der Werke rõmischer Bildhauerei mit der Namen des Künstler selbst, findet sich von der Statuen ein sehr mittelmässigen Äskuepius im Hause Verospi, an dessen Sockel der Name des Künstlers Assalectus stehet". Johan Winckelmann, *Sammtliche Werke, Geschichte de Kunst*, 8, ed. by Joachim Eislein, Donauöschingen, O. Zeller, 1825-1835, p. 270.

55. Ovid, *Fasti*, I, line 291.

56. Krautheimer, *Rome*, p. 180; Claussen, *Magistri Doctissimi*, p. 125 and n. 712.

57. The youthful head with notably projecting ears on the north side architrave of the cloister at San Paolo may be derived from a portrait bust of the Emperor Claudius. Here, as elsewhere in the architrave heads, the eyes have lead pupils. The right eye of the Antinous in the Banco d'Italia bears evidence of drilling, perhaps for the insertion of a metal pupil. Statues of Antinous generally have blank eyes; Smith, *Antinous*, p. 24, suggests that engraved iris lines or pupil markings become common only after c. 130 BCE, that is, after the creation of the official iconography of Antinous.

5. Ancient Rome in the Insular Experience

Our mainly clerical visitors did not only pursue their business at the curia, but likely also spoke with English residents and certainly picked up gossip on the current situation in the city. All of them, however, also turned to available sources of information, first and foremost the *Mirabilia urbis Romae*, an amorphous compilation that took various forms as it developed.[1] The earliest text so far recovered has a *terminus ante quem* of 1143, established by a reference to the imperial porphyry sarcophagus of Hadrian that was reutilised for the tomb of Pope Innocent II († 24 September 1143).[2] The first section of the *Mirabilia* was innovatory in its categorisation of buildings, and its catalogue of monuments was widely influential.[3] Gerald made considerable reference to it, Gervase also relied on it and its influence is also clearly detectable in Gregory's *Narracio*, although the latter is far more independent in its approach.

Gerald was assiduous in recording the physical dimensions of the great churches. But this practice is secondary to his informed interest in the status and dedication of these churches and their relics.[4] His account of the Lateran begins with the venerated wooden altar. He correctly notes that the Lateran was a church of papal privilege where no one should presume to celebrate, save the pope himself. Gerald buttressed his opinion through diligent reference to authentic records. He had, after all, come to Rome specifically to rummage in the papal archives. All altars in the Lateran, he noted, were subordinate to the principal, patriarchal altar, embellished with bronze plates and a ciborium, which allegedly saw the baptism of the Emperor Constantine and Saint Helena.[5]

1. Nine Robintje Miedema, *Die "Mirabilia Romae". Untersuchungen ihre Überlieferung mit Edition der deutschen und niederländischen Texte*, Tübingen, Niemeyer, 1996. See also the important review by Franz Josef Worstbrock, "Zeitschrift für deutsches Altertum und deutsches Literatur", 126/1 (1997), pp. 116-130; Dale Kinney, "Fact and Fiction in the *Mirabilia Urbis Romae*", in *Roma Felix: Formation and Reflections of Medieval Rome*, ed. by Éamonn Ó Carragain and Carol Neuman de Vegvar, Aldershot, Ashgate, 2007, pp. 235-252; Maurizio Campanelli, "Monuments and Histories: Ideas and Images of Antiquity in Some Descriptions of Rome", in *Rome across Time and Space*, pp. 35-59.

2. Kinney, "Fact and Fiction", pp. 235-236; *Le Liber Censuum de l'Église Romaine*, p. 385; Herklotz, *Gli eredi*, p. 19.

3. Campanelli, "Monuments and Histories", p. 36.

4. Herklotz, *Gli eredi*, p. 167.

5. *GC Opera*, vol. IV, p. 273. Oftestad, *The Lateran Church in Rome*, pp. 119-102.

Its New Testament relics surpassed those of the Old in importance. They included the seamless robe that Mary made for Christ, blood and water from the Crucifixion, fragments from the loaves and fishes, Christ's shroud and much else.[6] Interestingly enough, Gerald makes no mention of Christ's sandals, whose existence was to be hotly disputed at the end of the 13th century, a striking example of the politicisation of relics.[7] The heads of both Peter and Paul were preserved in the dependent church of San Lorenzo *in palatio* (the *Sancta sanctorum*).

He begins his account with the Lateran as foremost among the five principal churches of Rome. It had regular canons under a prior, whereas the Vatican had canons with a cardinal as archpriest. San Paolo was now a Cluniac monastery with an abbot. Then followed Santa Maria Maggiore and San Lorenzo *fuori le mura*, which had monks of the same congregation as at San Paolo, but with separate and distinctive prerogatives. Pre-eminent, despite the complaints of the Vatican canons, was the Lateran, the basilica of the Saviour, with dedications to Saint John the Baptist and Saint John the Evangelist. Thus, through this dedication, the Lateran was truly "caput et vertex omnium ecclesiarum".[8] At the end of the 13th century, this dedication was illustrated in Jacopo Torriti's apse mosaic, the very place where the image of Christ had first manifested itself to the Roman populace.[9]

Shortly afterwards, Constantine built Saint Peter's. Where Saint Peter's was pre-eminent, not only in Rome but throughout the whole world, was in the number of its lamps, of which 160 burnt daily.[10] This church stands next to the temple of Apollo and the Palace of Nero, two monuments that characteristically attracted the attention of Master Gregory. The body of the Apostle was in the altar, and above it was a ciborium borne by four porphyry columns.[11] In front of this stood the twelve marvellous spiral columns decorated with vine-leaves and putti brought from Greece, which were once part of the Temple of Apollo in Troy.[12] In a striking image, Gerald describes the procession for the great litany as in the form

6. *GC Opera*, vol. IV, p. 275.

7. Franz Pelster, "Eine Kontroverse zwischen englischen Dominikanern und Minoriten über einige Punkte der Ordensregel", *Archivum Fratrum Praedicatorum*, 3 (1933), pp. 57-80.

8. See p. 50 above. *GC Opera*, vol. IV, bk IV, ch. II, p. 272.

9. "Et imago Salvatoris depicta parietibus primum visibilis omni populo Romano apparuit". *GC Opera*, vol. IV, bk IV, p. 276; Alessandro Tomei, *Iacobus Torriti Pictor*, Rome, Argos, 1990, pp. 77-79.

10. *GC Opera*, vol. IV, p. 270: "…tum etiam beati quoniam Petri basilica caeteras ecclesias omnes urbis et orbis transcendit lumine lampadarum".

11. *Chronica Johannis de Oxenedes*, ed. by Henry Ellis, London, Longman, Brown, Green, Longmans and Roberts, 1859, p. 264 (1284): "Illa pars ecclesiae sancti Petri Romae ubi fuit altare Apostolo(rum)[?] cum praecipuis et principalibus iconibus subito corruit". Julian Gardner, *Cardinal Stefaneschi and Giotto* (forthcoming).

12. These columns still exist and were, with one exception, re-used by Bernini in New St Peter's. Alexis Gauvain, "La Colonna Santa Museo Storico Artistico del Tesoro di San Pietro", *Archivum Sancti Petri Bollettino d'Archivio* 28-29; Petrus Mallius stated that all 12 Constantinian gifts and "*de templo Apollinis Troiae*", but his source is unknown.

of a ship with the clergy of Saint Peter's in the bow with the pope as principal steersman at the stern.[13] The ship of the church could assume many forms.

Like the tomb of Peter, strongly bound in copper and bronze, the body of Saint Paul was buried deep in his church on the Via Ostiensis. Very strikingly, Gerald included the dimensions of Saint Peter's. It is difficult to use these dimensions, as it is unclear where the nave and transept were measured and whether the thickness of the walls were included.[14] The width of the atrium was 72 feet. The rafters of the roof are very long, almost 34 feet, and come from a special forest north of the city from whence they were floated down the Tiber.[15] Like Gerald before him, Gregory was a quantifier. He measured the Pantheon, once the temple of all the Gods. He paced its width and recorded it as 266 feet – a finding at odds with both actuality and received tradition. The internal diameter is actually 148 Roman feet, that is 43.80 metres.[16]

Disappointingly, apart from this somewhat abstract interest in physical dimensions, our visitors made no observations about the interior of the great rotunda at the turn of the 13th century. There is some slight visual documentation of what they could have seen. It is contained in a 16th-century drawing now in Milan's Muso Civico, which documents what is obviously a medieval ciborium (Fig. 17).[17] The slight sketch reveals a canopy design of 12th-century

13. *GC Opera*, vol. IV, p. 280: "Tum scilicet quoniam in majori Litania clerus sancti Petri, tanquam navis prora et aliorum vexillifera omni, de navi tota, hoc est de processione generaliter collecta praecedit, domino papa, tanquam principali et praecipue gubernatore, velut ex puppa sequenta".

14. *GC Opera*, vol. IV, p. 283: "Sciendum quod longitudo ecclesiae sexies XX passus (et) IX continet: longitudo vero crucis ecclesiae XX passus et duos; latitudo navis ecclesiae circiter LXXX passus; longitudo paradisi extra ad atrium et ecclesiae introitum LXXII. Item longitudo ecclesiae Sancti Pauli novies XX passuum et V; latitude vero corporis ecclesiae quantum XX passuum et X".

15. *GC Opera*, vol. IV, p. 263: "Notandum et hoc quoque quod in ecclesia beati Petri sunt trabes longissimae in latitudinem inter pilas et columnas porrectae. Scinduntur autem in sylva quadam quasi per VI miliaria ab urbe distante ex parte boreali, quae dicitur Missa beati Petri [...] Quod trabes illas scindunt quae abietinae sunt, et usque in Tiberim quqe non procul inde currit...".

16. *Magister Gregorius*, ed. by Huygens, ch. XXI: "Huius domus latitudinem ipse mensus sum habebat spacium CCLXVI pedum in latitudine". Nardella, *Il fascino*, p. 162; *Master Gregorius*, ed. by Osborne, p. 78. For the dimensions, see *The Pantheon from Antiquity to the Present*, ed. by Tod Marder and Mark Wilson Jones, Cambridge, Cambridge University Press, 2015, p. 16.

17. Arnold Nesselrath, "Impressions of the Pantheon in the Renaissance", in *The Pantheon*, pp. 255-295: 269. However, Antonio Muñoz discovered fragments of this ciborium in 1911: Antonio Muñoz, "La decorazione medioevale del Pantheon", *Nuovo Bullettino di Archeologia Cristiana*, 18 (1912), pp. 25-35: 30 and tav. V. He further demonstrated that the architectural fragment with the inscription INNOCENTIVS was reused, and might be referred more plausibly to Innocent III who consecrated an altar to St Laurence there in 1208. See Vincenzo Forcella, *Iscrizioni delle chiese e di altri edificii di Roma dal secolo XI fino ai giorni nostri*, 14 vols, Rome, Tipografia delle scienze matematiche e fisiche, 1869-1884, vol. I, p. 297, no. 1132 with the erroneous date of 1209. The altar was consecrated by Petrus Gallocia, cardinal-bishop of Porto; the correct year is calculated from Innocent's pontificate: Maleczek, *Papst und Kardinalskolleg*, p. 96, n. 284. The drawing is in Milan, Musei Civici, Gabinetto dei disegni, Raccolta Martinelli,

type where the rectangle provided by the four supporting columns around the altar is replicated at the next level, before being modified into an octagon, which is then itself crowned with a pyramidical roof. Similar structures survive from Sant'Andrea in Flumine at Ponzano Romano, and there are still comparable ciboria in Rome at San Lorenzo *fuori le mura* and San Giorgio in Velabro.[18] The medieval ciborium within the Pantheon was almost certainly similar.

Despite this taste for enumeration, Gerald was laconic about the physical appearance of the ancient monuments. It was a profound change of outlook from his earlier, careful scrutiny of Caerleon. No other 13th-century observer of Rome was capable of his former archaeological accuracy. Gervase is more sporadic, and often more formulaic. Nonetheless, his personal experience of antiquity and his attitude towards the ancient past can be documented in surprising contexts. Otto IV was an ineffectual emperor, distrusted and finally excommunicated by Innocent III, who, after his catastrophic defeat at Bouvines in July 1214, retired to the Kingdom of Arles. There, Gervase, who bore the title of imperial marshal, arbitrated a dispute over Les Alyscamps, one of the largest accessible collections of ancient sarcophagi known to the Middle Ages. A document dated 13 June 1221 confirms that the cemetery remained in active use, and the arbitrators were named as Raymond, Provost of Arles, and Master Gervase "in regno Arelaten imperialis aule marescalli" ("marshal in the imperial court in the kingdom of Arles").[19]

Gerald carefully described the icon of Christ in the *Sancta Sanctorum*, which he termed *Uronica*.[20] Despite its now illegible condition, it has been the subject of numerous studies.[21] Gerald's account is of great interest in that it

vol. V, f. 99r., illustrated in p. 270, fig. 9.7. The papal restoration of the ciborium was documented by inscription: for the modification of the altar disposition by Innocent VIII Cybo (1484-1492) in 1491, see Lanciani, *Storia degli Scavi di Roma*, vol. I, p. 88 and Forcella, *Iscrizioni*, vol. I, no. 1114. Early 16th-century drawings of the interior are discussed by John Shearman, "Raphael, Rome and the Codex Escurialensis", *Master Drawings*, 15 (1977), pp. 107-146: 109-117.

18. The Ponzano ciborium is signed by Nicolaus with his sons Iohannes and Guito: Claussen, *Magistri Doctissimi*, pp. 45-46, fig. 51. For San Giorgio in Velabro, see Claussen, Mondini, Senekovic, *Die Kirchen der Stadt Rom*, 3, pp. 15-58, ciborium pp. 50-56. Muñoz, "La decorazione", p. 28 suggested the ciborium at S. Lorenzo *fuori le mura* as a formal comparison: Claussen, *Magistri Doctissimi*, pp. 16-17 and fig. 11.

19. Albanès, *Gallia Christiana Novissima*, no. 2628, 13 June 1221. A judgement two days before had been in favour of Eldiardis abbess S. Césaire "...super absolutione cimiterii de Aliscampis [...] cum libera sepultura illorum qui ibi sepeliebantur", no. 873, col. 343, 4 June 1221. Duprat, "Histoire des Légendes Saintes de Provence", pp. 118-198; 18 (1941), pp. 87-186: 108 [1941] prints, pp. 153-157, full text of 11 June 1221 arbitration, which mentions "arcas corporibus humanis aptissimas de saxis ingentibus noviter fecit incidi, quas per omne pavimentum basilice constipatas sterni fecit ordine, ut quecumque congregationis illius de hac luce migrasset, locum sepulture paratissimum et sanctissimum reperiret..." in S. Césaire.

20. *GC Opera*, vol. IV, p. 278: "una Romae habetur apud Lateranensem scilicet in sancta sanctorum". Gerald describes it as "tota cooperta [...] auro et argento toto praeter genu dextrum a quo oleum indesanter emanat". The revetment has a hole at the right knee to accommodate this effusion.

21. This painting has been the subject of many studies since Wilpert was first permitted to examine it: Josef Wilpert, "L'Acheropita, ossia l'immagine del Salvatore nella Cappella

totally ignores the then current belief that it was completed by an angel. He states that it was painted at Mary's suggestion by Saint Luke, "pictor quoque mirabilis". After many deletions and corrections, it was accepted by the Virgin as an accurate likeness.[22] This icon was carefully set above the altar when Nicholas III rebuilt the palatine chapel in 1278-1279.[23] Gervase also refers to this panel: "There is also another image of the Lord's features, this one imprinted in a similar miraculous way on a panel in the oratory of St Lawrence in the Lateran Palace. A pope of our time Alexander III (1159-1181), of holy memory, had it covered with a large silk cloth, because it caused such violent trembling in people who gazed at it too intently that there was a risk of death".[24] Contemporaneously, Gerald, in his *Speculum ecclesiae*, recounted comparable precautions at Saint Peter's.[25]

The silver revetment with which the *Sancta sanctorum* Christ was enclosed is probably to be seen as a comparable prophylaxis. It has proven a problematic work. Generally dated to the end of the 12th century, a recent critic noted its archaising style, "un gusto vistosamente conservatore".[26] More plausible is a substantially earlier date, and there are several strong arguments for the view that it was made some forty years earlier. In its *repoussé* technique and ornamental repertoire, it is very similar to a reliquary now in the parish church at Ponzano Romano but which originally came from the nearby abbey of Sant'Andrea in Flumine.[27] This reliquary,

del Sancta Sanctorum", *L'Arte*, 10 (1907), pp. 161-177, 247-262; Gerhard Wolf, *Salus populi romani*, Weinheim, VCH Acta Humaniora, 1990, pp. 39-40; Michele Bacci, *Il pennello dell'evangelista: storia delle immagini sacre dedicati a San Luca*, Pisa, GISEM, 1998, *ad indicem*: Serena Romano, "L'icône *achieropiete* du Latran. Fonction d'une image absente", in *Art, Cérémonial et Liturgie au Moyen Âge, Actes du colloque de 3e Cycle Romand de Lettres, Lausanne-Fribourg, 24-25 mars, 14-15 avril, 12-13 mai, 2000*, ed. by Nicholas Bock, Peter Kurmann, Serena Romano and Jean-Michel Spieser, Rome, Viella, 2002, pp. 301-320; Herbert Kessler, "Christ's Dazzling Dark Face", in *Intorno al Sacro Volto. Genova, Bisanzio e il Mediterraneo (XI-XVI secolo)*, ed. by Anna Rosa Calderoni Masetti, Colette Dufour Bozzo and Gerhard Wolf, Venice, Marsilio, 2007, pp. 231-246: 231.

22. *GC Opera*, vol. IV, p. 278: "Cum ergo ipsa indicante prius singular membra pinxisset, et post multarum deletionum corrections, tandem in unam imaginem conjuncta matri obtulisset, ipsa imaginem diligentius intuita sujunxit 'Hic est filius meus'".

23. Julian Gardner, "'L'architettura del *Sancta Sanctorum*", *Sancta Sanctorum*, ed. by Carlo Pietrangeli, Milan, Electa, 1995, pp. 19-38: 20.

24. Gervase of Tilbury, *Otia Imperialia*, p. 606: "Et est alia dominici vultus effigies, in tabula eque impressa, in oratorio sancti Laurentii in palatio Lateranensi, quam sancte memorie nostri temporis papa Alexander tertius multiplici panno serico operuit, eo quod attentius intuentibus tremorem cum mortis periculo inferret".

25. *GC Opera*, vol. IV, p. 279: "Haec (scil. Veronica) in magna similiter reverentia: et a nemine, nisi per velorumquae ante dependent inter positionem inspicitur: et haec est apud Sanctum Petrum". Wolf, *Salus Populi Romani*, p. 277, n. 366.

26. Antonio Iacobini, "Le Arti del Metallo: Oreficeria e Bronzi", in *Roma nel Duecento, L'arte nella città dei papi dall'Innocenzo III a Bonifacio VIII*, ed. by Angiola Maria Romanini, Turin, Ed. Seat, 1991, pp. 306-319: 310-313. It consists of 6 pieces silver nailed together and gilt. The saints are related to relics chapel. The current shutters are Quattrocento replacements.

27. Giuliana Zandri, "No. 15 Reliquario, Ponzano Romano from S. Andrea in Flumine", *Mostra d'Arte Sacra di Roma e del Lazio dal Medioevo all'Ottocento, Palazzo delle Esposizione*

which shows the Enthroned Christ on the obverse, has the same embossed foliate and stellar decoration as the Roman revetment. The small standing saints that frame the Enthroned Christ have the same jerky animation as those on the Lateran revetment.[28] It is signed by Rainerius Teramnese, a toponym most likely identifiable with Terni in Umbria. Relics of St Andrew, the abbey's patron, are mentioned in the inscription. The abbey of San Andrea had a sumptuous refurbishment of its liturgical furniture by the Cosmati workshop, headed by a certain Nicolaus, in collaboration with his sons Iohannes and Guittone, who left their inscription beside the *fenestella* of the *confessio*. This ensemble has been dated to around 1160.[29] Thus, the suggested dates of both the Lateran silver revetment and the reliquary of Sant'Andrea would coincide with the pontificate of Alexander III, to whom Gervase of Tilbury ascribes the veiling of the icon. Alexander's enthusiasm for metal work is documented: a commission for twenty-four candlesticks and a gilt cup are recorded.[30] Had the revetment been very recently commissioned by Innocent III, whose curia Gerald was then petitioning, it is surely unlikely he would have omitted to mention the fact.[31] Innocent, in fact, showed a marked personal preference for Limoges enamel-work.[32]

The anonymous English Franciscan who visited Rome in the mid-1340s reported that similar precautions were taken for the Virgin icon at Santa Maria in Trastevere: "the image of the Blessed Virgin, which St Thomas of Canterbury held in veneration while he was there, and now has the face covered by a cloth for no Christian would dare look on it uncovered".[33] This description of veiling the Madonna panel is all the more interesting as it is virtually contemporaneous with a requirement in the will of cardinal Annibale da Ceccano, who founded a college annexed to the basilica. Every Saturday after lectures, the students were to go to the church and sing an antiphon in front of the sacred image, and their teacher

Novembre – Dicembre, 1975, pp. 11-12, tav. XII, XIII: silver 15x15x6, signed by Ranerius of Terni (?). RAINERIUS TERAMNESE FE(CIT) (H)O(C) OPVS. Zandri gives the full inscription on p. 11.

28. Iacobini, "Le arti del metallo", figs pp. 311-313.

29. +NICOLAV CVM FILIIS IOANNES ET GVITTONE FECERUNT HOC OPVS. Claussen, *Magistri Doctissimi* p. 45 and fig. 50. A lost inscription on the high altar at the Duomo of Sutri by the same workshop included the date 1170. Claussen, *Magistri Doctissimi*, p. 47.

30. "…candelabra xxiv et cuppam xiv marcarum deauratam intus et extra": Philipp Jaffé, Samuel Löwenfeld, *Gesta Pontificorum Romanorum*, Leipzig, Veit, 1885-1888, no. 13035 (March 1178); Gardner, *Roman Crucible*, p. 158, n. 10.

31. The report must come from an early recension of the *Speculum*. Gerald continually revised his writings. First adumbrated circa 1191, since it is alluded to in the *Itinerarium Kambriae*, it was not completed until late in Gerald's career, for it mentions both the fall of Constantinople to the Franks (1204) and the Lateran Council of 1215, and its preface was added even later: Bartlett, *Gerald of Wales: A Voice of the Middle Ages*, p. 179; Richard W. Hunt, "The Preface to the *Speculum Ecclesiae* of Giraldus Cambrensis", *Viator*, 8, (1977), pp. 189-213.

32. Gardner, *The Roman Crucible*, pp. 157-160.

33. "…sancta Marie transtyberim, Sancte Marie, ubi est ymago beate Virginis quam sanctus Thomas Cantuariensis habuit in veneration, dum ibidem fuerat, que nunc habet faciem quodam panniculo velatam, in quam nudam aspicere non audit ullus christianus." Golubovich, *Biblio Bio-Bibliogafica*, p. 440; *Western Pilgrims*, p. 53.

was to say a prayer.[34] Gerald mentions yet another image bearing Christ's features "non depicto sed ligno magis insculpto" ("not painted, but rather carved"), which was to be seen at Lucca in Tuscany.[35]

Earlier, we noted how closely Gerald examined Roman domestic construction at Caerleon. We know less about the earlier experience of Roman monuments in the case of Gervase, although his service in Otto's household certainly brought him into close contact at some stage with the impressive Roman ruins at Arles, and working for William II of Sicily must have provided him with a glimpse of other ancient vestiges in southern Italy. Of the prior experiences of antiquity by our most perceptive and voluminous commentator on ancient Rome, Master Gregory, we know virtually nothing.[36] None of them, however, could ever have experienced anything on the scale of the ruined monuments they were to see in Rome.

Gregory, in his introductory praise of the Roman cityscape, unobtrusively employed the rhetorical device of inexpressibility, describing an "uncountable thicket" of urban towers, "tanta seges turrium".[37] This rhetorical ploy was subverted by a slightly later English author. In his *Chronica majora*, Matthew Paris made the matter-of-fact comment that the Senator Brancaleone degli Andalò razed 140 towers: "...he destroyed the towers of the Roman nobles and imprisoned their owners. Indeed, many kinsmen and familiars of the cardinals were hanged or mutilated".[38] About a century later, the anonymous 14th-century English Franciscan remarked on "sculptures and likenesses in bronze and stone, which are so many and so various that no Christian might describe them".[39] These timid images of incomparability differ considerably from the concrete comparisons made by Ludolf, rector of Sudheim, whose account of his travels, written in 1350, habitually compared the size of the rivers he encountered to his native Rhine, or fountains to those in his native Paderborn.[40] The church on Calvary, he opined, was similar to churches in Westphalia, especially in their choir arrangements. Mount Tabor was very similar to Dezenberg in the diocese of Paderborn.

34. Marc Dykmans, "Le cardinal Annibal de Ceccano (vers 1282 – 1350), étude biographique et testament du 17 juin 1348", *Bulletin de l'Institut Historique Belge de Rome*, 43 (1973), pp. 145-344: 296, "Item singulis diebus sabbati, cum demiserint lectiones, vadant ad ecclesiam Beate Marie in Transtiberim et coram ymagine domine nostre cantent antiphonam unam, et prior vel magister dicat unam orationem beate Virginis".

35. *GC Opera*, vol. IV, p. 279. It was originally brought from Constantinople by a bishop of Lucca.

36. See p. 14 above.

37. Ernst R. Curtius, *European Literature and the Latin Middle Ages*, London, Routledge, 1953, pp. 159-162; Campanelli, "Monuments and Histories", p. 42.

38. *Matthaei Parisiensis Monach Sancti Albani Chronica Majora*, vol. V, ed. by Henry R. Luard, London, Longman & Co., 1880, p. 723: "...dirui fecit turres nobilium circiter centum et quadraginta...".

39. Golubovich, *Biblioteca Bio-Bibliografica*, p. 441: "...columpnis marmoreis eversis, de conchis marmoreis ad instar navicularum: de columpnis, ostiis, statuis hominum et bestiarum variis ymaginibus, sculpturis et simulacris, eneis et saxeis, quot sunt et quomodo se habent, nullus scriberet christianus".

40. See p. 30, note 5 above.

Master Gregory characterised Rome's pyramids as tombs of the mighty – "sunt autem piramides sepulcra potentum" – alluding perhaps to Gaius Cestius, although the "pyramid" of Julius Caesar, in his opinion, deserved the greatest admiration (Figs 18-19). This, in fact, was a granite obelisk, the only one that stood throughout the Middle Ages and that now occupies the pride of place in the Vatican piazza, where it was successfully moved and re-erected by Domenico Fontana. It is, Gregory noted, "made of a single porphyry block. It is indeed a marvel how a block of stone of such height could have been cut, or have been raised, or remain standing, for they say its height is 250 feet".[41] Until the 15th century, it was believed to be supported on four lions, and it is shown thus in the mural at San Piero a Grado outside Pisa.[42] Only when the base was subsequently cleared was the myth discredited.[43] The interest in the ancient obelisks appears to have been widespread in the period, as Cosmati masons erected a fragmentary obelisk in front of Santa Maria in Capitolio around 1200.[44] Gregory was contemptuously dismissive of the pilgrims' fable that the pyramid of Cestius was the granary of Saint Peter, "an utterly worthless tale, typical of those told by pilgrims".[45] Contemporaneously, however, the third Joseph cupola mosaic, which was executed in the first half of the 13th century in the atrium of San Marco in Venice, explicitly labels them as Joseph's Horrea.[46] Gregory restricted himself to a crisp description of its structure and function: "of enormous size and height, rising to a point in the manner of a cone [...] Hidden inside every pyramid is a marble sarcophagus, with carved reliefs on all sides, in which the body of the deceased was placed".[47]

Classical authors, however, did not provide medieval visitors with the foundational reading for identifying the bronze equestrian monument, then located near the Lateran (Fig. 20) as either Marcus or Quintus Quirinus, rather than its popular ascription as Constantine, the first Christian Roman emperor, although this

41. "Sunt autem Rome piramides multe set omnium maiori admiracione Digna est piramis Iulii Cesaris, que ex uno solisoque lapide porfi(ri)co condita est". Nardella, *Il fascino*, p. 168; *Master Gregorius*, ed. by Osborne, pp. 88-89; Erik Iversen, *Obelisks in Exile*, vol. I, *The Obelisks of Rome*, Copenhagen, Gad, 1968, pp. 19-46. A 16th-century drawing attributed to Baldassare Peruzzi shows it standing on four orbs. *GC Opera*, vol. VIII, p. 208 describes it as "*numidici lapis*".

42. Jens Wollesen, *Die Fresken von San Piero a Grado bei Pisa*, Bad, Oeynhausen, 1977, pp. 60-72: 67-68 and fig. 28.

43. Iversen, *Obelisks in Exile*, p. 26.

44. Ronald E. Malmstrom, "The Twelfth Century Church of S. Maria in Capitolo and the Capitoline Obelisk", *Römisches Jahrbuch für Kunstgeschichte*, 16 (1976), pp. 1-16.

45. *Master Gregorius*, ed. by Osborne, p. 33; Nardella, *Il fascino*, p. 168: "Quod omino frivolum est, quo peregrini multum habundant".

46. Demus, *The Mosaics of San Marco*, vol. II, pp. 88-166 and fig. 295. Burchard of Mount Sion describes the pyramids as such: "...quedam piramides triangule multum alte, qui dicuntur horrea Iosep fuisse...", in *Descriptio Terrae Sanctae*, ed. by John R. Bartlett, Oxford, Oxford University Press, 2019, p. 216. See p. 81 below.

47. Nardella, *Il fascino*, p. 168: "Sunt autem piramides [...] mire magnitudinis et altitudinis in summitate acute, figuram hec conoidis referents [...] Habet autem piramis quelibet concam marmoream undique celatam infra se clausam in qua corpus defuncti sepelitur".

identification was firmly denied by the *Mirabilia*. There were no extensive accounts of Marcus Aurelius, and the *Silvae* of Statius, whose poem on the *equus Domitiani* still lay undiscovered in a German monastic library near the Lake of Constance,[48] was found and copied by Poggio Bracciolini in 1417.[49] The *Mirabilia* attempted to "explain" the monumental group but yields little substantive information.[50] Gregory devoted more space to it than any other topic. The *Liber Pontificalis* in the biographies of Popes John XIII (965-972) and John XIV (983-984) had identified it as the *caballum Constantini* and as Constantine in front of his *Basilica salvatoris*, and thus it would echo in Statius' "Par operi sedes".[51]

Yet, despite his intense interest, Gregory did not venture an opinion on what was one of the profoundest visual paradoxes of the sculpture itself, an unarmed intellectual astride a warhorse. For many medieval observers, the incongruity generated much false aetiology. Intellectual superiority was an elevated form of *auctoritas*, and the plausible representation of learned and venerable prelates on their tombs was an incipient problem for the 13th-century sculptor. It is of course Gregory, who not only provides the modern reader with the best information about the fate of the Marcus Aurelius in the early 13th century, but who also furnished precious information about other classical sculptures he examined during his Roman visit.

Gregory's *Narracio* has aspects that relate it to the ancient genre of *laus civitatis*.[52] Like William of Malmesbury, he cites the great poem of Hildebert of Lavardin (1096-1125): "Equal to you, Rome, there is nothing, though you be nearly a total ruin. Broken, you teach how great you were whole. Long ages have destroyed your pride, and the fortresses of Caesar, and the temples of the gods lie in the swamp".[53] But his gaze is far wider and more sceptical. Insufficient attention has, however, been paid to other textual aspects, yet he also leans substantially on the *Graphia aureae urbis Romae* of around 1185, the oldest re-working of the *Mirabilia* that gave an imperial cast to a text which, it has been

48. Statius, *Silvae*, ed. by David R. Shackleton Bailey, Cambridge (MA), Harvard University Press, 2003, pp. 20-38; Dale Kinney, "The Horse, the King and the Cuckoo: Medieval Narrations of the Statue of Marcus Aurelius", *Word and Image*, 18 (2002), pp. 372-398: 372.

49. Statius, *Silvae*, p. 7; Kinney, "The Horse", p. 376.

50. Gerlinde Huber-Rebenich, *Mirabilia Urbis Romae. Die Wunderwerke der Stadt Roms*, Freiburg-im-Breisgau, Herder, 2014, pp. 90-94. Dale Kinney, "*Mirabilia Urbis Romae*", in *The Classics in the Middle Ages*, ed. by Aldo Bernardo and Saul Levin, Binghampton (NY), Center for Medieval and Early Renaissance Studies, 1990, pp. 207-221 notes the *Mirabilia* "author's peculiar understanding of Roman antiquities as oracular texts in which the record of Providence could be read by those who knew how..."

51. Statius, *Silvae*, p. 32. See also *Le Liber Pontificalis*, 2, pp. 252, 259; *Master Gregorius*, ed. by Osborne, p. 44. The attempt to identify the original location of the monument by Valnea Santa Maria Scrinari, *Il Laterano imperiale*, Città del Vaticano, Pontificio Istituto di Archeologia Cristiana, 1991-1997 has met with scepticism. See Herklotz, *Gli eredi*, pp. 214-215. Herbert Mielsch, "Review of *Santa Maria Scrinari*", *Bonner Jahrbuch*, 193 (1993), pp. 514-516.

52. For later manifestations, see Kenneth Hyde, "Medieval Descriptions of Cities", *Bulletin of the John Rylands Library*, 48/2 (1968), pp. 308-344.

53. *Master Gregorius*, ed. by Osborne, p. 18.

persuasively argued, emerged from the "republican" atmosphere of Rome in the 1140s.[54] Gregory consistently, and unusually, attempted to provide explanations for the buildings he described. His almost casual references to cardinals, with whom he apparently consulted directly, nonetheless reveal something of his elevated status as a visitor: "I shall give a wide berth to the worthless stories of the pilgrims and the Romans […] and shall record what I have been told by the elders, the cardinals and the men of the greatest learning".[55] He also sifted through the information he received, preferring learned opinion, and at times confessing his own shortcomings: "In front of [the Capitoline wolf] […] there is a bronze tablet […] on which are written the principal statutes of the law. On the tablet I read much but understood little, for they were aphorisms and the reader has to supply most of the word*s*".[56] (One of Cola di Rienzo's achievements was to read the *pataffi*.)[57] This is surely not the sentiment of a parodist.

Gregory carefully described the gestures of the Marcus Aurelius: "The rider raises his right hand as if to address the people or to give orders: his left hand holds a rein, which turns the horses head to the right".[58] He was equally precise in describing the marble (probably that now in the Capitoline Museums) in a celebrated passage. Both are examples of *ekphraseis*: "This image is made from Parian marble with such wonderful and intricate skill, that she seems more like a living creature than a statue; indeed she seems to blush in her nakedness, a reddish tinge colouring her face and it appears to those who take a close look that blood flows in her snowy lips. Because of this wonderful image, and perhaps because of some magic spell of which I was unaware, I was drawn back three times despite the fact that it was 2 *stades* from my inn".[59] Here the emphasis is on the aesthetic effect, whereas the detailed description of the gigantic bronze head in front of the Lateran focuses on its technical perfection.

The assessment of the beauty or preciousness of objects was already one of the innovations of the *Mirabilia*. But there, these qualities were attributes of

54. Herklotz, "Der Campus Lateranensis", pp. 26-28.

55. *Master Gregorius*, ed. by Osborne, p. 20. Nardella, *Il fascino*, p. 148: "Ceterum peregrinorum et Romanorum super hac re vanas fabulas penitus declinabo eamque originem huius operis assignabo quam a senioribus et cardinalibus et viris doctissimis didici".

56. Gregory is the first to mention the bronze wolf. Nardella, *Il fascino*, p. 172: "Ante hanc enea tabula est, ubi pociora legis precepta scripta sunt […] In hac tabula plura legi set pauca intellexi. Sunt enim afforism(i), ubi fere omnia verba subaudiuntur". Anonimo Romano, *Cronica*, ed. by Giuseppe Porta, Milan, Adelphi, 1979, p. 143.

57. Anonimo Romano, *Cronica*, p. 143 (Cola): "Tutta die se speculava nelli intagli di marmo li quali iaccio intorno a Roma. Non era aitri che esso, che sapessi leiere li antiqui pataffi". Ida Calabi Limentani, "Sul non saper leggere le epigrafi classiche nei secoli XII e XIII: sulla scoperta graduale delle abbreviazioni", *Acme*, 23 (1970), pp. 253-282; Herklotz, "Der Campus Lateranensis", pp. 21-23.

58. *Master Gregorius*, ed. by Osborne, pp. 19-20; Nardella, *Il fascino*, p. 146: "Sedet autem eques manum dexteram dirigens tanquam populo loquens vel imperans; sinistra manu frenum retentat, quo capud equi in dexteram partem obliquat, tanquam alio diversurus".

59. *Master Gregorius*, ed. by Osborne (modified Mary Carruthers, *The Experience of Beauty in the Middle Ages*, Oxford, Oxford University Press, 2013, p. 194, n. 49). Camille, *Gothic Idol*, pp. 83-84, who uses Osborne's translation.

Christian buildings, too, and helped explain the outstanding beauty of Rome, which was conceived of as a sacred space more than a city.[60] This was not the case with Gregory, who used the great churches mainly as indicators of location. There was something magical in a statue's power to affect him.[61] Gregory's sense of the supernatural aspect of Rome is a particularly interesting dimension of his reaction to the antique. It is quintessentially medieval rather than humanistic. The standing figure of Venus, now in the Capitoline Museums, is often considered to have been the object of Master Gregory's enthusiastic description (Fig. 21).[62] Whether that is the case or not, there can be little doubt that he was at least commenting on a comparable figure.

A brilliant reflection of a 4th-century original from the circle of Praxiteles, the goddess is shown bathing prior to her marriage to Hephaistos. The slender nuptial *loutrophoros*, over which her garment is laid, identifies the moment, when we and her other visitor intrude. Her elaborate coiffure is in elegant disarray, and a slight smile flickers on her lips, as an implicit intruder disturbs her privacy.[63]

The contemporary accessibility of the Capitoline Venus for Gregory's enjoyment is, however, problematic. It was found in the gardens of the Stazi family near San Vitale on the Viminale in 1666-1667. The statue was subsequently purchased by Benedict XIV (1740-1758), who presented it to the Capitoline Museums in 1752. But the circumstances of its finding are revealing; it appears to have been walled up, perhaps as a protection, some time during the medieval period.[64] In his description of the statue, Gregory alludes directly to the Judgement of Paris in Ovid's *Ars amatoria*. Slightly later in the same poem is the couplet that has led modern scholars to identify it with a Venus in the collection of Gaius Asinius Pollio (76 BCE – 41 CE), a collection the poet knew well.[65] Were that to be the case, it would be a

60. Campanelli, "Monuments and Histories", pp. 38-39.

61. Erwin Panofsky, *Renaissance and Renascences in Western Art*, Stockholm, Almqvist & Wiksells, 1960, p. 112 inexplicably characterises this reaction as "uneasiness". See Jane L. Long, "The Survival and Reception of the Classical Nude: Venus in the Middle Ages", in *The Meanings of Nudity in Medieval Art*, ed. by Sherry C. Lundquist, Burlington (VT), Ashgate, 2012, pp. 47-64: 63, n. 42.

62. Ch. 12; *Master Gregorius*, ed. by Osborne, p. 26. Intriguingly, his description clearly alludes to *Ars Amatoria* I, 248: "Cum dixit Veneri 'vincis utramque Venus'". Ovid, *The Art of Love and Other Poems*, transl. by John H. Mozley, revised by George P. Goold, Cambridge (MA), Harvard University Press, 1978, p. 30.

63. Andrew Stewart, "A Tale of Seven Nudes: The Capitoline and Medici Aphrodites, Four Nymphs at Elean Herakleia and Aphrodite at Megalopolis", *Antichthon*, 44 (2010), pp. 12-32. Hadrianic period, 193 cms high. The original is c. 330-310 BCE. There is an elaborate analysis of Gregorius' description in Camille, *The Gothic Idol*, pp. 84, who suggests the influence of classical *ekphrasis*.

64. Lanciani, *Storia degli Scavi di Roma*, vol. II, pp. 47-48: "la bella venere di marmo pario che hanno in casa i Signori Stati, cavalieri romani". Haskell, Penny, *Taste and the Antique*, no. 84, pp. 318-320 and fig. 169.

65. Gregory, evidently quoting from memory, gives "Iudicio nostro vincit utranque Venus". The poem reads "Cum dixit Veneri," "vincis utranque Venus". Ovid, *The Art of Love and Other Poems*, transl. by John H. Mozley, rev. by George P. Goold, Cambridge, MA, Harvard University Press, 1979, Lib. II, lines 613-614: "Ipsa Venus pubem, quotiens velamina

high-quality copy of a Praxitelean original, which was certainly in Rome in the 1st century CE, perhaps as part of Sulla's booty from Piraeus and Athens.[66]

Gregory's breath was taken away by the sculptor's craftsmanship and the life-likeness of the sculptured goddess. It is its imitation of life that is exceptional. Although Ovid's *Ars amatoria* comes unbidden to his mind, it is its beauty, not its sexuality, that drew Gregory back.[67] So beautiful is it that he returned to gaze at it thrice, not because of some kind of magical persuasion that he could not understand, but because of its artfulness.[68]

There was also another classical statue, the *Spinario* or thorn-puller, a sculpture also widely imitated but whose meaning in this period remains uncertain (Fig. 22).[69] Gregory, in a famous passage, derided it as "ridiculoso simulacro", an inadequate Priapus: "There is another bronze statue, a rather laughable one, which they call Priapus. He looks as though he is in severe pain, with his head bent down as if to remove from his foot a thorn that he had stepped on. If you lean forward and look up to see what he's doing, you discover genitals of extraordinary size".[70] This is perhaps intended as ironic, and thus another example of Master Gregory's familiarity with ancient rhetoric. Certainly, prudery was not part of his repertoire.[71] Whether it is to be considered as parodic, however, is quite another matter. What is certain is that Gregory's

ponit / Protegitur laeva semireducta manu". Ovid's phrase certainly encapsulates the complex movement of the Roman figure. Stewart, "A Tale of Seven Nudes", p. 18.

66. Antonio Corso, "L'Afrodite Capitolina e l'arte del Cefisodoto il giovane", *Quaderni ticinesi di numismatica e antichità classiche*, 21 (1992), pp. 131-157; Antonio Corso, *The Art of Praxiteles*, vol. II, *The Mature Years*, Rome, Bretschneider, 2007, pp. 25, 82; Stewart, "A Tale of Seven Nudes", p. 18.

67. *Master Gregorius*, ed. by Osborne, p. 26, n. 7.

68. Nardella, *Il fascino*, p. 158: "...nescio quam magicam persuasionem...". I adopt the compelling interpretation of Carruthers, *Experience of Beauty*, pp. 194-195.

69. Osborne, *Rome in the Eighth Century*, p. 155; Serafin Moralejo Alvarez, "Marcolfo, el Spinario, Priapo un testimonia iconografica gallega", *Prima Reunion de Estudios Clasicos (Santiago - Pontevedra) 2 – 4 julio 1979*, Santiago, 1981, pp. 331-359. Haskell, Penny, *Taste and the Antique*, no. 78, pp. 308-310.

70. "Est etiam aliud eneum simulacrum, valde ridiculosum, quod Priapum dicunt. Qui dimisso capite velud spineam calcatam educturus de pede, asperam lesionem pacientis speciem representat. Cui si quid agat exploraturus suspexeris mire magnitudinis virilia videbis." Nardella, *Il fascino*, p. 154. Gerald and Innocent III could also share an arch joke about testicles. *GC Opera*, vol. III, pp. 253-254. There is a drawing by Mabuse, who was in Rome in 1508-1509, from exactly this viewpoint. See Marion Ainsworth, *Man, Myth and Sensual Pleasures: Jan Gossart's Renaissance, the Complete Works*, New Haven, Yale University Press, 2010, pp. 45-55, figs 47, 48; Stiegemann, *Wunder Roms*, p. 408, no. 77. Gunther Schweikhart, "Von Priapus zu Coridon", *Würzburger Jahrbücher für Altertumswissenschaft*, N.F.3 (1977), pp. 243-252: 244. It recurred often as a calendar figure for March, p. 245. Slightly modified and clothed it is reflected in Filippo Brunelleschi's competition relief for the Florentine Baptistery doors; Richard Krautheimer, in collaboration with Trude Krautheimer-Hess, *Lorenzo Ghiberti*, Princeton, Princeton University Press, 1970, pp. 44-49: 45.

71. Dale Kinney has suggested that it was the nudity of the classical statuary that forced medieval observers to a new level of interpretation. Kinney, "The Horse", p. 388.

text was intended for a limited, cultivated audience, whereas the *Mirabilia* was widely popular and known to many.[72]

Interest in the iconography of ancient theatrical masks can be discerned among the architrave heads of the cloister of the Lateran, which had been commissioned by a cardinal from southern Italy, Pietro da Capua.[73] Gervase reports an extremely interesting episode, which must have taken place earlier, the only episode any of our observers report as occurring well beyond the walls of Rome. Gervase had earlier connections with southern Italy, from when he was a familiar of William II of Sicily (1153-1189). A year after William's death, he visited his former pupil Giovanni Pignatelli, the Archdeacon of Naples. Gervase possessed a summer house (*mansio*) at Nola, some 30 kilometres distant from Naples, an earlier gift William II "ob declinandos Panormitanos tumultus ac fervores estivos" ("escape the noise and bustle of Palermo in the summer"). He records in his *Otia imperialia* how Pignatelli explained the impact on travellers of two sculptured heads set on either side of the Porta Nolana at Naples, one lamenting, the other rejoicing:

> he showed us a head of Parian marble inserted in the wall of the gateway on the right-hand side, with its mouth stretched into a merry laugh of immense delight. But on the left-hand side there was another head affixed to the wall of the same marble, but otherwise very different from the first for it presented the face of someone weeping, wild-eyed and angry, and bewailing the hardship of a wretched lot.[74]

As with Gregory, the adjective "Parian" was synonymous with fine white marble.[75] The heads were evidently ominous and, depending on which one the wayfarer encountered first, they conditioned his fate. Should he observe the tragic mask first, his future would be unfortunate, but if he saw the comic one, it was benign.

72. As witnessed still by the modern edition by Huber-Rebenich, *Mirabilia.*

73. Peter Cornelius Claussen, "Scultura romana al tempo di Federico II", in *Federico II e l'Arte del Duecento italiano, Atti della III Settimana di Studi di Storia dell'Arte Medievale dell'Università di Roma (15-20 Maggio 1978)*, vol. I, ed. by Angiola Maria Romanini, Galatina, Congedo Editore, 1980, pp. 325-338: 334. Stephen Halliwell, "The Function and Aesthetics of the Greek Tragic Mask", in *Intertextualiät in der griechisch-römischen Komödie*, ed. by Niall Slater and Bernhard Zimmermann, Stuttgart, M & P Verlag, 1993, pp. 195-211: 204-207; Michael Walton, "Actors, Chorus and Masks", in *The Art of Ancient Greek Theater*, ed. by Mary L. Hart, Los Angeles, J. Paul Getty Museum, 2010, pp. 33-41.

74. Gervase of Tilbury, *Otia Imperialia*, p. 580: "Accedentibus nobis ostendit in dextra parte caput parieti portalis insertum de marmore Pario, cuius rictus ad risum et eximie iocunditatis hylaritem trahebantur. In sinistra vero parte parieti erat aliud caput de consimili marmore infixum, sed altere valde dissimile: oculis siquidem torvis, flentis vultum ac irati, casusque infelicis iacturam plorantis pretendebat. Ex his tam adversis vultuum imaginationibus duo sibi contrario fortune proponit archidiaconus omnibus ingredientibus imminere…".

75. Carruthers, *Experience of Beauty*, p. 194, n. 50. For white Parian statuary marble, see Ben Russell, *The Economics of the Roman Stone Trade*, Oxford, Oxford University Press, 2013, pp. 83-84, 180. Gerald describes the fountain by the Lateran where he conversed with Innocent III as made of Parian marble. *GC Opera*, vol. III, p. 252: "fons pulcherrimus […] Pariis lapidibus arte conclusus…". He confers with cardinals Pietro da Capua and Soffred when present with the Curia at Segni: *GC Opera*, vol. III, p. 191.

What is remarkable about this episode is that it clearly refers to a pair of ancient theatre masks that had been set in the city wall flanking the gate as *spolia* (Fig. 23). This is a generation earlier than Frederick II's epoch-making gate at Capua, itself indebted to classical city gates. It is a practice that can contemporaneously be documented in medieval city gates elsewhere in Italy.

The restored Aurelianic gates added to the original city walls of Rome were, on occasion, decorated with statues, and images of Honorius and Arcadius were added to the Porta Tiburtina. Such programmes could be celebratory of the ruler's achievements, or minatory, aimed at discouraging opponents. An important surviving medieval example is found in the Porta Consolare at Spello in Umbria, where three classical standing figures are added rather crudely to the external face of the gate (Fig. 24).[76] The triple entrance of the gate is also clearly inspired by a triumphal arch of the type of the Arch of Constantine. Such arches might indeed be integrated into the city wall itself, as was the case at Rimini, and other examples can be found elsewhere in communal Italy.[77] The Capuan Gate of Frederick II, now reduced to an ungainly stump, when complete was a summation of both these traditions: it was a gate with a decorative sculptural programme that celebrated a living ruler. But the use of ancient *spolia* to emphasise a civic identity, as at Naples, is unusual. Clearly, the explanation Giovanni Pignatelli provided for Gervase would have been classified by the hard-headed Gregory among the empty fables fed to pilgrims. Nonetheless, Gervase thought it worthy of record. And it is an important early witness to the reception of classical *spolia* in medieval southern Italy.

76. Julian Gardner, "An introduction to the Iconography of the Medieval Italian City Gate", *Dumbarton Oaks Papers*, 41 (1988), pp. 199-213: 209 and fig. 4.

77. Diana Kleiner, "The Study of Roman Triumphal and Honorary Arches 50 years after Kähler", *Journal of Roman Archaeology*, 2 (1989), pp. 195-206.

Illustrations

1. Manorbier Castle, Pembrokeshire, Wales.
2. Lindisfarne Gospels, c. 700 CE. British Library Cotton Nero D IV, f. 26v.

3 

5 

3. Llanthony, Augustinian Priory. Monmouthshire, Wales.

4

4. Caerleon, Roman Arena, 90 CE. Monmouthshire, Wales.
5. Rome, view from Monte Mario, c. 1499. Monastero di San Lorenzo el Real Escorial Biblioteca, Sign. 28-II-12, ff. 7v.-8r.

6. Rome, Septizonium, 203 CE. Hieronymus Cock, *S*erie Praecipua Aliquot Romanae Antiquitatis Ruinarum Monumenta. Kunstsammlung der Georg-August-Universität Göttingen.
7. Rome, Campus Lateranensis. Maarten van Heemskerck Sketchbook c. 1532-1536. Kupferstichkabinett, Staatliche Museen zu Berlin, Inv. -Nr. 79 D2. ff. 12r., 71r.

8. Bronze Wolf, Fifth Century BCE. Rome, Musei Capitolini, N. MC 1181.
9. Bronze Ram, First Half Third Century BCE. Palermo, Museo Nazionale Archeologico, N. 8365.

10. Bronze head of Constantine, c. 330 CE. Rome, Musei Capitolini, MC 1072.

11. Antonio Eclissi (fl. c. 1630-1644). Mural formerly in the apse of the Oratory of St. Nicholas, Lateran Palace. Windsor, Royal Library 8981.

12. Innocent III. Fragment of the Apse Mosaic of Old Saint Peters 1205-1212 CE. Museo di Roma.

13. Rome, San Paolo fuori le mura. Honorius III. Detail of the Apse Mosaic. Early Thirteenth Century.

14. Rome, San Paolo fuori le mura. Vassalectus, Cloister, West Wall, Early Thirteenth Century.
15. Rome, San Lorenzo fuori le mura, Cloister, Late Twelfth Century.

16. Antinous, Second Century CE. Rome, Banca d'Italia, Palazzo Koch, Inv. No. 14424.

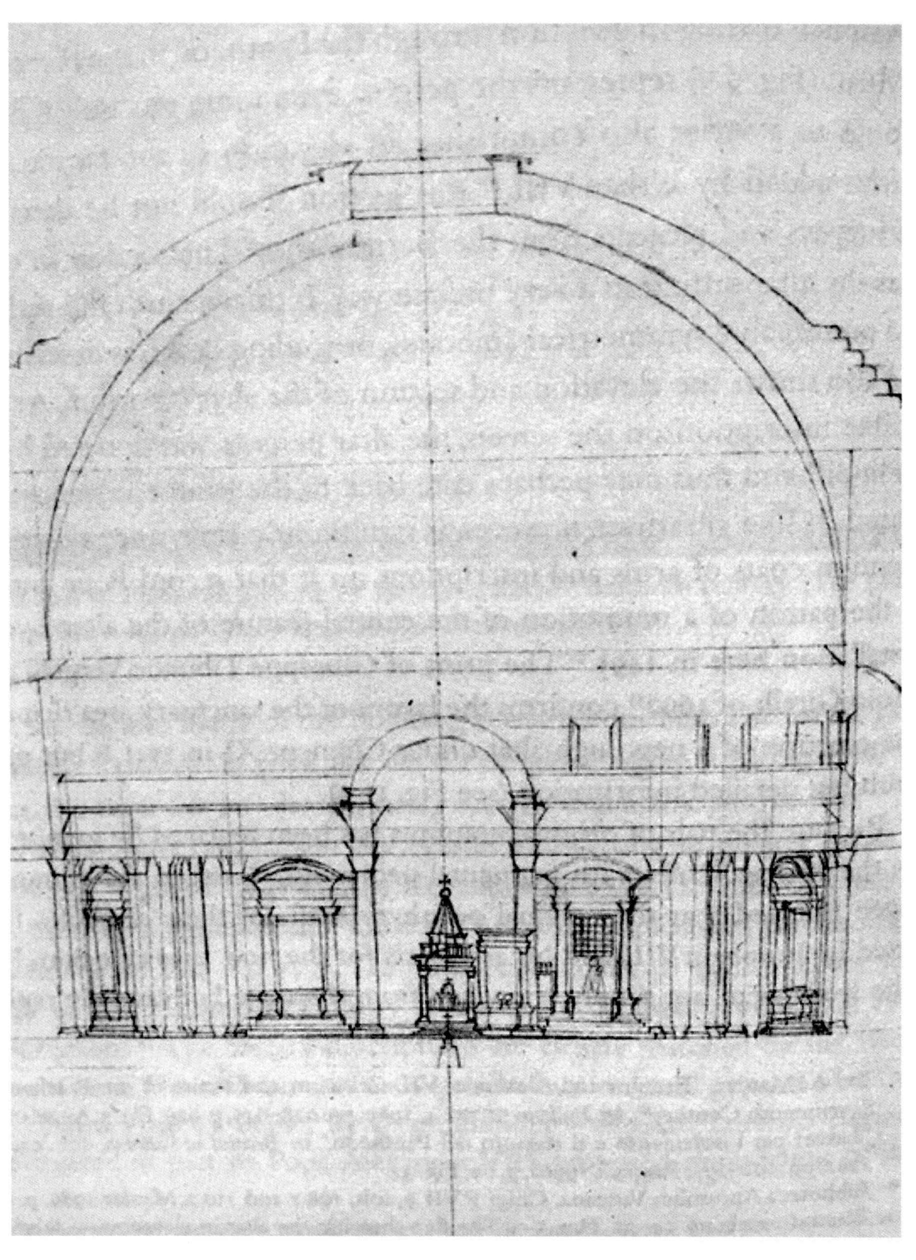

17. Interior of the Pantheon. Milan, Civico Gabinetto dei Disegni, Raccolta Martinelli, vol. V, f. 99r.

18. Rome, Pyramid of Gaius Cestius, c. 18-12 BCE.
19. Rome, Obelisk. Maarten van Heemskerck Sketchbook c. 1532-1536. Kupferstichkabinett Staatliche Museen zu Berlin, Inv. -Nr. 79 D2. f. 7r.

20. Equestrian Statue of Marcus Aurelius, 161-180 CE. Rome, Musei Capitolini, N. MC 3247.

21. Venus, Second Century CE. Antonine copy of Praxitelean model. Rome, Musei Capitolini.

22. Spinario, First Century CE. Rome, Musei Capitolini N.MC 1186.
23. Ancient Theatre Mask. Rome, Museo Nazionale Romano. Muses sarcophagus, Late Third Century CE, Inv. 80711.

24. Spello (Umbria), Porta Consolare, c. 42 BCE.
25. Rome, Pantheon, Façade. Maarten van Heemskerck Sketchbook c. 1532-1536. Kupferstichkabinett, Staatliche Museen zu Berlin, Inv. -Nr. 79 D2. f.10 r.

26a-b. Città del Vaticano, Museo Gregoriano Egizio, Lions of Pharoah Nektanebo II, 358-340 BCE.

27. Rome, Santi Apostoli. Bassalectus, Lion, Early Thirteenth Century.
28a-b. Anagni, Duomo. Vassalectus, Paschal Candelabrum, c. 1260.

29a-b. Rome, S. Giovanni in Laterano, Cloister, South Walk. Vassalectus, Sphinxes, c. 1230.

30. Rome, S. Giovanni in Laterano, Cloister, West Walk, Lion, c. 1230.
31. Cività Castellana, Duomo, Drudus and Lucas, Sphinx, c. 1240.

32. Ferentino, Duomo, Drudus, Sphinx, c. 1240-1250.
33a-b. Rome, S. Giovanni in Laterano, Vassalectus, Cloister, Architrave, Details.

34. Rome, Sant'Antonio Abbate, Portal, Sphinx, c. 1260.

35. Fra Pascalis OP, Sphinx from S. Maria in Gradi, 1286. Viterbo, Museo Civico.

6. In the Shadow of the Pantheon: Isis in Rome

Master Gregory's sharp eye for classical sculpture is well known. He was almost obsessed with obelisks, a subject virtually ignored by earlier accounts. The obelisks of Rome were, in general, imperial imports from Egypt.[1] He was also the first witness to the ancient sculptures set in front of the Pantheon: "I shall only briefly mention the Pantheon, once the idol house of all the gods, or rather of all the demons. This building is now a church dedicated in honour of all the saints, although it is generally called S. Maria Rotonda. It has a spacious portico, supported by many lofty columns, and in front of it there remain to this day a basin and other wonderful porphyry vessels, as well as lions and other statues made of the same material" (Fig. 25).[2] He also mentions the pyramids, which remained a feature of the Roman cityscape: "piramis Iulii Caesaris quae ex uno solidoque lapide porfirico condita est" ("the one which deserves the greatest admiration is the pyramid of Julius Caesar, made of a single porphyry block").[3] So, in relatively few words, he referred to one of the most surprising phenomena of Roman sculpture and cloister architecture of the period – the arrival of Egyptomania.[4]

1. Iversen, *Obelisks in Exile*, pp. 11-18; Anne H. M. Roullet, *The Survival and Rediscovery of Egyptian Antiquities in Western Europe from Late Antiquity until the Close of the Sixteenth Century*, Ph.D. Dissertation, Oxford, 1969, pp. 22-24. See also Brian Curran, *The Egyptian Renaissance: The Afterlife of Ancient Egypt in Early Modern Italy*, Chicago, University of Chicago Press, 2007.

2. Nardella, *Il fascino*, p. 162: "Ante quam conche et vasa alia miranda de marmore porfirico et leones et cetera signa de eodem marmore usque in hodiernum diem perdurant". *Master Gregorius*, ed. by Osborne, p. 29, 34. Gregory makes no mention of the closure of the intercolumniations, rather like what one can still observe at the Lateran Baptistery, which had also occurred at the Pantheon at an earlier date. See Michael Viktor Schwarz, "Eine frühmittelalterliche Umgestaltung der Pantheon-Vorhalle", *Römisches Jahrbuch der Bibliotheca Hertziana*, 26 (1990), pp. 1-29; Thunø, "The Pantheon in the Middle Ages", pp. 248. These barriers had certainly been removed by the 16th century.

3. *Master Gregorius*, ed. by Osborne, p. 34.

4. Karl Noehles, "Die Kunst der Cosmaten und die Idee der Renovatio Romae", in *Festschrift für Werner Hager*, ed. by Günter Fiensch and Max Imdahl, Recklinghausen, Bongers, 1966, pp. 17-27: 25 ff.; Rudolph Wittkower, "Hieroglyphics in the early Renaissance", in *Developments in the Early Renaissance. Papers of the Second Annual Conference of the Center for Medieval and Early Renaissance Studies, State University of New York at Binghampton, 4-5 May 1968*, ed. by Bernard S. Levy, Albany, 1968, pp. 58-97.

Gregory's observations raise some important questions about contemporary discoveries in Rome. He was specifically referring here to the basalt lions of Pharaoh Nektanebo II, which are now in the Vatican Museums (Fig. 26).[5] These were unequivocally pagan monuments from classical Rome. Egyptian lions could readily enough be adapted for an episcopal throne, such as that of Bishop Lando at the Duomo of Anagni, made by Vassallettus on the biblical model of the throne of Solomon.[6] The impact of the Nektanebo lions on Cosmati sculpture was profound. More ancient Egyptian and Egyptianising artefacts have been found in the close neighbourhood of the Pantheon and Santa Maria sopra Minerva than anywhere outside Egypt. By the second half of the 1st century CE, Isaac religion had firmly established itself in Rome, and the emperor Domitian himself rebuilt the *Iseum Campense* after a fire in 80 CE.[7] There appears to have been a surge of rediscovery in the early 13th century, perhaps through increased building activity in the area, although the nearby construction of the Dominican church of Santa Maria sopra Minerva comes too late to explain this.[8] The tradition reported by Flaminio Vacca, which stated that they were excavated under Pope Eugenius IV, lacks foundation.[9]

The lions are characterised by heads turned at 90 degrees, neat ears and short, orderly manes, which frame their faces like a ruff.[10] The similarity of pose and facial characterisation can be seen in a considerable number of Cosmati lions, beginning perhaps with the one now set in front of Santi Apostoli, which is inscribed on its base with BASSALLECTVS (Fig. 27).[11] These similarities would seem to prove without doubt that the Pharaonic lions outside the Pantheon served as models for contemporary Roman sculptors, and were indeed those that Gregory noted in his *Narracio*.

5. Josef Deér, *The Dynastic Porphyry Tombs of the Norman Period in in Sicily*, Cambridge (MA), Harvard University Press, 1959, p. 109; Anne Roullet, *The Egyptian and Egyptianizing Monuments of Imperial Rome*, Leiden, Brill, 1972, p. 7. See now Katja Lembke, *Der Iseum Campense in Rom: Studie über den Isiskult unter Domitian*, Heidelberg, Verlag Archäologie und Geschichte, 1994, pp. 223-224, nos 13-14; Luchterhand, "*Mirabilia* – Die Antiken Roms", p. 108.

6. II Paralipomenon, ch. 9, vv. 17-19: "…duos leones stantes iuxta brachiola…". Claussen, *Magistri Doctissimi*, pp. 122-125, figs 139, 144. The throne bears two inscriptions. PRESVL HONORANDUS OPVS HOC DAT NOMINE LANDVS is around the rim of the marble halo-like disk that forms the upper back of the throne, and the sculptor's signature, VASALETo DE ROMA ME FECIT, is just below it. Noehles related the throne to that in the apse of Santa Maria in Cosmedin: Noehles, "Die Kunst der Cosmaten", p. 24.

7. Lembke, *Der Iseum Campense*, pp. 137-138.

8. Ursula Kleefisch-Jobst, *Santa Maria sopra Minerva: Ein Beitrag zur Architektur der Bettelorden in Mittelitalien*, Münster, Nodus Publikationen, 1991, pp. 25-33.

9. Flaminio Vacca, *Memorie di varie antichità trovate in diversi luoghi della città di Roma scritte ...nell'anno 1594,* in Flaminio Nardini, *Roma Antica*, 2nd ed., Rome, Ottavio Falconieri, 1704.

10. Deér, *The Dynastic Porphyry Tombs*, p. 107.

11. Claussen, *Magistri Doctissimi*, pp. 112-115; Noehles, "Die Kunst der Cosmaten", p. 28 suggests that it might have had a candelabrum between its forepaws, rather as the Paschalis candelabrum at Santa Maria in Cosmedin. This, however, would seem to pose problems of scale.

There is no certainty about the model or models that inspired the Cosmati sculptors' sphinxes.[12] They evince a greater diversity than do the lions. There is as much variety in the bodily forms as in the facial expressions. Crucially, they are often given the function of bearers of columns, be it in the great Roman cloisters, in the Paschal candelabrum at Anagni or elsewhere (Fig. 28).[13] Roman masons turned the mysterious expression of the original into a vacant rictus. Significantly enough, the Vassallectus workshop was also responsible for the lion outside Santi Apostoli. As with the lions of Nektanebo, the bases, which in the original bore explanatory hieroglyphs, became the place where the Roman medieval stone-carver placed his name.

Curial patronage of this contemporary Egyptianising sculpture can be traced in the early Duecento. Pietro da Capua, whose name features prominently on the cloister of San Paolo *fuori le mura*, was an influential cardinal with whom Gervase of Tilbury conferred in Rome in 1209, and who showed his English visitor an incombustible strap made of salamander skin: "I myself saw, when I was lately in Rome, a strap of salamander skin about the size of a belt which had been brought there by the cardinal Master Peter of Capua. When it had picked up some dirt from being handled, it was put into a fire, and before our eyes the fire cleansed it of every stain but did not burn it at all".[14] Gerald also conferred with him and Cardinal Soffred at Segni.[15]

Cardinal Pietro had, in 1212, already commissioned a cloister for regular canons at San Pietro a Tozzolo, near Amalfi.[16] The inscription on the cloister architrave records Pietro's name at San Paolo, during the abbacy of Giovanni da Ardea. The inscription has been restored but originally read:

HOC OPUS ARTE SUA QUEM ROMA CARDO BEAVIT
NATUS DE CAPUA PETRUS OLIM PRIMITIAVIT

12. Possible Roman models are suggested in a pioneering discussion by Manuela Gianandrea, "Creazioni à l'antique. I Vassaletto e il fascino della sfinge egizia nel medioevo romano", *Hortus Artium Medievalium*, 16 (2010), pp. 151-159: 154-155. Paired sphinxes flanked the entrance to Diocletian's mausoleum at Split. Roullet, *Egyptian and Egyptianizing Monuments*, p. 5, n. 1.

13. Heinz Demisch, *Die Sphinx Geschichte ihrer Darstellung von den Anfängen bis zur Gegenwart*, Stuttgart, Urachhaus, 1977, p. 57. Sphinxes as column bases already 13 BC. For the Anagni candelabrum, see Claussen, *Magistri Doctissimi*, pp. 122-124, figs 140, 143. It is signed VASSALETO ME FECIT. Sphinxes also support columns in the Lateran cloister and the corner colonnette of the displaced choir screen at Cività Castellana.

14. Gervase of Tilbury, *Otia Imperialia*, vol. III, pp. 558-560. Gervase's information about the Salamander probably derives from Pliny, *Natural History*, X, 6. Kinney has characterised this kind of explanation as "novelistic aetiology": Kinney, "The Horse", p. 385.

15. Gerald conferred at Segni with Pietro da Capua and Soffred, cardinal-priest of Santa Prassede. Maleczek, *Papst und Kardinalskolleg*, pp. 73-76; *GC Opera*, vol. III, 191, 195.

16. Werner Maleczek, *Petrus Capuanus Kardinal, Legat am vierten Kreuzzug, Theologe († 1214), Publikationen des Historischen Instituts beim Oesterreichischen Kulturinstitut in Rom, 1. Abt. Bd.8*, Vienna, Österreichischen Akademie der Wissenschaften, 1988, pp. 222-224, 306-311; *Die römische Kurie und das Geld. Von der Mitte des 12. Jahrhunderts bis zum frühen 14. Jahrhundert (Vorträge und Forschungen LXXV)*, ed. by Werner Maleczek, Ostfildern, J. Thorbeke, 2018, pp. 118-124; Gardner, *Roman Crucible*, p. 41.

ARDEA QUEM GENUIT QUIBUS ABBAS VIXIT IN ANNIS
CETERA DISPOSUIT BENE PROVIDA DEXTRA IOHANNE[17]

The Benedictine cloister was a project of the Vassallectus workshop, and was completed by 1214. The monastery of San Paolo had been taken in hand by Honorius III, who was also responsible for the completion of the apse mosaic. He insisted on observance of the rule. This admonition seems to have been observed, if with little enthusiasm.[18] The Benedictine cloister was more austere than the cloister at the Lateran, and no sphinxes were included, although some hybrids with sphinx-like characteristics are visible at the base of the great Paschal candelabrum signed by Nicolaus de Angelo and Pietro Vassalletto.[19]

The slightly later cloister at San Giovanni in Laterano was also a product of the Vassallectus shop, and it is this monument that contains important testimony of the sculptor's role in this "Egyptian revival". The cloister architrave carries a lengthy inscription, which has been restored on numerous occasions and can be reconstituted only by reference to early antiquarian sources.[20] It exhorts the canons to live the truly religious life.

Paired sphinxes appear prominently at the centre of the south walk of the Lateran cloister, where they are differentiated by age – a distinctly un-Egyptian feature (Fig. 29). The sphinx on the southwest side of the entry into the cloister has the head of a mature man with vigorously curling hair, a full beard and a serene facial expression. The younger sphinx on the southeast side is beardless and has a slightly vacuous grin. Both are male with a lion's body, and they wear the ceremonial head covering over the hair. They gaze inwards toward the cloister walk. All three other entrances are flanked by seated lions. Only the paired lions at the western entrance show the influence of Egyptian lions (Fig. 30). The impact of the lions of Nektanebo is much more strongly marked in the lions carved by Vassallectus at the sides of the

17. Fedele, "L'iscrizione del Chiostro di San Paolo", pp. 269-276. See also Ermenegildo Scaccia Scarafoni, "Il chiostro di S. Paolo fuori le mura: la sua epigrafe musiva e una notizia cassinese inedita", *Le Arti*, 5 (1942), pp. 11-15.

18. Brentano, *Rome before Avignon*, p. 223.

19. Noehles, "Die Kunst der Cosmaten", p. 26 and p. 35, n. 43 who also links the candelabrum with the new Cosmati cloister. See also Claussen, *Magistri Doctissimi*, pp. 108-109; Fabrizio Biferali, "Ridicula monstruositas? Spunti iconografici sul chiostro dei Vassalletto in San Paolo fuori le mura", *Arte Medievale*, 4 (2005), pp. 45-57.

20. It was already in a poor state when transcribed by Onofrio Panvinio, *De praecipuis Urbis Romae sanctioribusque basilicis quas septem ecclesias vulgo vocant liber*, Rome, 1570, pp. 173 ff.; Claussen, Mondini, Senekovic, *Die Kirchen der Stadt Rom im Mittelalter 1050-1300*, Bd. 3, pp. 259-273. An expanded and corrected version is given by Stefano Riccioni, *Il mosaico absidale di S. Clemente a Roma. Exemplum della chiesa riformata*, Spoleto, Centro Italiano di Studi sull'alto Medio Evo, 2006, p. 8, n. 65. It reads "Canon(icam) formam sumentes discite nor(m)am / quam pr(o)misis(tis h)oc c(lau)strum (quando) petistis. / Discite sic e(sse t)ria vo(bis nec)esse: / nil p(ro)prium morem castum portare pudorem./ Claustri structura sit vobis docta figura / ut sic clarescant anime moresq(ue) nitescan(t) / et s(tabiliant)ur animo qui canonicantur / ut coniunguntur lapidesq(ue) sic poliuntu(r) / gaudeat (in coelis [...] (christo) q(ue) [...] (fi) idelis / qui sua demisit operi vel m(und)i...", in Claussen, Mondini, Senekovic, *Die Kirchen der Stadt Rom*, 3, p. 262, n. 1178.

episcopal throne at Anagni. The other pair on the eastern walk at the Lateran cloister are crouching in a distinctively medieval posture.[21]

The external face of the south cloister walk was prominently signed by Vassallectus:

NOBILIT' DOCT HAC
VASSALLECTUS I ARTE
CU' PATRE CEPIT OPVS QD SOL' PERFECIT IPE

This inscription carefully (and surely deliberately) is placed to the left of the entrance to the eastern (?) walk of the cloister so that the mason's own name appears beneath the CLAUSTRI of the architrave inscription.[22] It also provides the important information that the skilled mason (*doctus in arte*) began the work in collaboration with his father, but finished it alone. Foreign visitors to Rome could hardly but be struck by the glittering polychromy of its decoration. A slightly later English visitor, Abbot Richard de Ware of Westminster, arranged for Cosmati masons to contribute to the sanctuary of his abbey and to the shrine of the royal saint entombed there. The materials for the mosaic decoration at Westminster were necessarily imported from Rome.[23]

In 1227, Cardinal Guala Bicchieri, who had served as a papal legate in England, and who was to construct a majestic cloister at his Victorine foundation in his native Vercelli, bequeathed in his will of 29 May 1227 10 lib. prov. *ad opus claustri Lateranensi*.[24] This suggests, but does not prove, that the cloister was still under construction at that date. The Lateran was a cathedral cloister, and thus fundamentally different in purpose from the Benedictine cloisters at San Paolo *fuori le mura* or San Lorenzo. As the cathedral of Rome, Saint John Lateran was serviced by canons who followed the Augustinian rule. But, as with so much in Rome, the position of the canons at the Lateran was singular. Despite forming the community of the bishop of Rome, they had no participatory rights in the election of the pope. Nevertheless, their role in the liturgies of great papal ceremonies was very prominent.

Sicard of Cremona († 1215), an influential commentator of the time, wrote in his *Mitrale* that there were four sides to a cloister.[25] One was disregard of self,

21. Noehles, "Die Kunst der Cosmaten", p. 27 suggests a link with Hellenistic-Roman models.

22. Expanded, it reads: "Nobiliter doctus hac Vassallectus in arte / cum cepit opus quod solus perficit ipse". Claussen, *Magistri Doctissimi*, pp. 126-132.

23. *Westminster Abbey, The Cosmati Pavements*, ed. by Lindy Grant and Richard Mortimer, Aldershot, Ashgate, 2002; Mathew Payne, Warwick Rodwell, "Edward the Confessor's Shrine in Westminster Abbey: Its Date of Construction Reconsidered", *Antiquaries Journal*, 97 (2017), pp. 187-204: 187-188; Tim Tatton-Brown, "The Two Great Marble Pavements in the Sanctuary and Shrine Areas of Canterbury Cathedral and Westminster Abbey", in *Historic Floors: Their Care and Conservation*, ed. by Jane Fawcett, Oxford, Butterworth-Heinemann, 2007, pp. 53-62.

24. Agostino Paravicini Bagliani, *I Testamenti dei Cardinali del Duecento*, Rome, Società Romana di Storia Patria, 1980 prints the will on pp. 110-118: 116, no. 22. Construction dates of 1225-1235 are suggested by Claussen, Mondini, Senekovic, *Die Kirchen der Stadt Rom*, Bd. 3, p. 261.

25. *Sicardi Cremonenses Episcopi Mitralis de Officiis*, ed. by Gabor Sarbak and Lorenz Weinreich, Turnhout, Brepols, 2008 (Corpus Christianorum Continuatio Medievalis, 228) vol.

the second *contemptus mundi*, the third *amor proximi*, and the last *amor Dei*. The columns of the cloister advocated humility, and their bases signified patience. This symbolic interpretation was reiterated, word for word, in Guillaume Durand's *Rationale Divinorum Officiorum* almost a century later, when the modern mendicant cloisters at Santa Maria in Aracoeli and Santa Maria sopra Minerva had already been constructed.[26] Pietro da Capua's inscription had laid out the purpose of the cloister at San Paolo: HIC STUDET ATQUE LEGIT MONACHORUM CETUS ET ORAT. At the Lateran, in contrast, we are not well informed of how the new cloister was used, despite the hortatory inscription. Numerous functions and ceremonial usages, such as vesting and ablutions, are described by the prior Bernhard in his mid-12th-century *Ordo Officorum Ecclesiae Lateranensis*. Guardian sphinxes like those at the Lateran clearly could have no Christian connotations.

The Cosmati workshops did not develop a model sphinx after the example of the lions imitating those of Nektanebo. Their ecclesiastical patrons did not have a biblical locus to which they could point. Equally so, our British spectators had no classical authority to guide them. It is nevertheless evident that a variety of Roman imitations were available to the Cosmati workshops in Rome for the purposes of imitation. Exceptionally, these medieval versions survive in their original contexts in a number of cases.

The earliest sphinx by the Cosmati mason Drudus de Trivio embellished the now dismantled choir screen at Cività Castellana, where it is accompanied by three lions (Fig. 31). The gently enigmatic smile of the Egyptian original has become a rictus. The psychological subtleties the smile had achieved contemporaneously in the monumental figure sculpture of northern European cathedrals is utterly remote.[27] The ostentatious choir screen bears an unobtrusive inscription that demonstrates that Drudus was working there together with a second mason.[28]

I/4, p. 23. For Sicard's career, see Edward Coleman, "Sicard of Cremona as Legate of Innocent III in Lombardy", in *Innocenzo III Urbis et Orbis*, vol. II, pp. 929-953: 940 ff.

26. *Gvillelmi Dvranti Rationale Divinorum Officiorvm*, ed. by Anselme Davril and Timothy M. Thibodeau, Turnhout, Brepols, 1995-2000, vol. I, ch. 1, no. 42, CXL, p. 25. The cloister at the Minerva was begun around 1280: Kleefisch-Jobst, *Die römische Dominikanerkirche Santa Maria sopra Minerva*, p. 25. In taking over a much older church of Santa Maria in Capitolio, the Franciscans inherited two cloisters: Claudia Bolgia, *Reclaiming the Roman Capitol: S. Maria in Aracoeli from the Altar of Augustus to the Franciscans c. 500-1450*, London, Routledge, 2017, pp. 87-88.

27. Willibald Sauerländer, "Vom Gelächter des Teuffels zur Ironie der philosophen. Über das Lachen im Spiegel der Bilder", *Zeitschrift für Kunstgeschichte*, 39 (1976), pp. 167-192; Paul Binski, "The Angel Choir at Lincoln and the Poetics of the Gothic Smile", *Art History*, 20 (1997), pp. 350-374.

28. DRVD' ET LVCAS CIVES ROMANI MAGRI DOCTISSIMI HOC OPVS FECERUNT: Claussen, *Magistri Doctissimi*, pp. 145-147. The lions show little relation to the Egyptian originals then accessible outside the Pantheon. For Drudus de Trivio, see Manuela Gianandrea, "Drudo di Trivio e Luca di Cosma gli artisti le opere e il loro intervento a Civita Castellana", in *La cattedrale cosmatesca di Civita Castellana, Atti del Convegno internazionale di studi (Civita Castellana 2010)*, ed. by Luca Creti, Rome, Bretschneider, 2012, pp. 217-232. I am very grateful to Dott.ssa Giandrea for making her publication available to me.

Here, the sphinx and three couchant lions guarded the entry to the presbytery. Only one of the lions, that on the right of the right-hand section of the screen, shows some faint impact of the Egyptian models then in front of the Pantheon. The Cosmati sculptors experimented with different head-coverings to conceal the difficult anatomical transition from human head to animal body.

A magnificent pair of sphinxes guards the sunny southern side entrance to the cloister at the Lateran.[29] One is young and clean-shaven, and the other majestically bearded. Like some of their Egyptian models, they support columns on their backs. They are certainly bearers of meaning, although the import within their new Christian context remains obscure to us.[30] The Lateran displays the most prominent sphinxes to remain in their original architectural context. They were clearly acceptable to regular canons but apparently not to the Benedictines of San Paolo. Those at Ferentino (Fig. 32) and Lanuvio lack their original contexts within their cathedrals, but very likely supported an elaborate choir screen like their counterpart at the Duomo of Cività Castellana.[31] The Duomo itself possesses a majestic portal façade, which is evidently influenced by Roman triumphal arches.[32] The decorative ensemble at Ferentino, signed by Drudus de Trivio, was a commission by Giovanni da Ferentino, at some time archpriest of the cathedral at Norwich and later cardinal.[33] The fragmentary sphinx at Lanuvio probably also once formed part of a Cosmati refurbishment, perhaps executed in conjunction with Vassallectus. It, too, very probably was part of a choir screen.[34] The Lanuvio

Elizabeth Freeman, "A Fountain Basin by Drudus de Trivio (fl c 1230-40): A Reconsideration", *Antiquaries Journal*, 99 (2019), pp. 105-132.

29. Claussen, Mondini, Senekovic, *Die Kirchen der Stadt Rom*, Bd. 3, pp. 297-302; there is one pair of sphinxes and three pairs of lions.

30. John Onians, *Bearers of Meaning: The Classical Orders in Antiquity, the Middle Ages and the Renaissance*, Princeton, Princeton University Press, 1988.

31. Claussen, *Magistri Doctissimi*, pp. 145; Manuela Gianandrea, "Drudo di Trivio e Luca di Cosma gli artisti le opere e il loro intervento a Civita Castellana", in *La cattedrale cosmatesca di Civita Castellana*, pp. 217-232: 223-224. Manuela Gianandrea, *La scena del sacro. L'arredo liturgico nel basso Lazio tra XI e XIV secolo*, Rome, Viella, 2006, pp. 145-146.

32. Noehles, "Die Kunst der Cosmaten", p. 30 postulates the so-called Arch of Galienus as a model.

33. Cheney, "John of Ferentino", pp. 654-656; Maleczek, *Papst und Kardinalskolleg*, pp. 147-148; Claussen, *Magistri Doctissimi*, figs 137, 211. The ciborium bears the inscriptions +ARCHIL'VITA FVIT NORWICI HAC URBE IOH'S EX GENC.: + MAGISTER DRVDV' DE TRIVIO CIVIS ROMANVS FECIT HOC OPVS. The front right ciborium capital is obviously based on a classical model: Gardner, *The Roman Crucible*, p. 109. See p. 76 below. The church furniture probably postdates Gerald's visit of 1206.

34. A fragment of an architrave is inscribed "...SSALLETTVS FECIT HOC OPVS ARCHIPRESBITERO IOhS". Alberto Galieti, "Memorie della chiesa medievale di Cività Lavinia", *L'Arte*, 12 (1909), pp. 349-358: 353 and fig. 3; Claussen, *Magistri Doctissimi*, pp. 119-120; Manuela Gianandrea, "L'Egitto dei faraoni nella Roma dei papi: riflessioni sull'Egitto nella cultura medievale tra storia, religione e mito", *La Lupa e le sfinge: Roma e l'Eitto dalla storia al mito, Mostra, Roma 2008*, ed. by Eugenio lo Sardo, Milan, Electa, 2008, pp. 132-142; Manuela Gianandrea, "Creazioni à l'antique. I Vassaletto e il fascino della sfinge egizia nel medioevo romano", *Hortus Artium Medievalium*, 16 (2010), pp. 151-159.

fragment is important from another point of view: an inscription recorded by Gualdi provides us with a secure date for the sculpture campaign, 1240. It once again confirms the family basis of the Cosmati workshops.[35]

The small paired sphinxes at Anagni, another work prominently signed by Vassallectus, who had also signed the throne of Bishop Lando, form the decorative support of an imposing Paschal candelabrum.[36] This ensemble contains the only three-dimensional figural sculpture by Vassallettus, the chubby Atlas figure who supports the upper candle basin. It is a wholly different concept from that of the relief figures that ornament the great candelabrum at San Paolo *fuori le mura*. The Anagni ensemble is probably the most thoroughly Egyptianising of the surviving lion groups. Even the six-pointed star in the disk at the back of the throne is probably derived from the Islamic decorative repertoire.

Several heads in the elaborately carved figural cornice of the Lateran cloister reveal an awareness of classical theatre masks, of the kind Gervase saw at Naples (Fig. 33). The reception and re-use of both antique models and Egyptianising motifs is characteristic of the workshop of Drudus de Trivio.[37] The magnificent, antique-inspired capitals on the ciborium at Ferentino confirm Drudus as one of the protagonists of classical revival in mid-13th-century Roman sculpture.[38] Drudus also signed the small fountain basin now in the Museo di Palazzo Venezia, which bears the extraordinarily obscure inscription +HIC THETIS ESCE PRIVS ABLVE MANDE QUIESCE ("Here is the water, hence the food, first wash it, eat it and repose"). Thetis is probably a confusion with Tethys, mother of all rivers, rather than her granddaughter Thetis, the mother of Achilles.[39] The classical allusiveness of the inscription conforms with the statues of Antinous and Aesculapeus mentioned earlier. Drudus was also, however, one of the pioneers of Egyptian-inspired sphinxes and lions in Rome and the surrounding area.

Paired sphinxes were set at the Mausoleum of Diocletian at Spalato.[40] The Egyptian sphinx was, in origin, a pharaoh's head set upon a lion's body.[41] The lion

35. Francesco Gualdi, *Epitaphia et insignia nobilium familiarum ecclesia Urbis*, Vat. Lat. 8253, f. 500. + A D MCCL EGO APB IOH SARACEN' F FI h' OP A MAGISTRO DRVDO ROMANO C ANGLO FILIO SUO. The archpriest Johannes Saracenus is not otherwise known. It is unlikely that the Johannes Saracenus mentioned in 1154 is the same person: Maleczek, *Papst und Kardinalskolleg*, p. 99, note 330.

36. Claussen, *Magistri doctissimi*, p. 122, figs. 140-143.

37. The name is uncommon: see Olof Brattö, *Studi di antroponimia fiorentina Il Libro di Montaperti (An. MCCLX)*, Göteborg, Elanders Boktrykerei, 1953, pp. 122-123 (Drudolus).

38. The Ferentino capitals may reflect a number of Roman models visible during the Middle Ages, for example those on the *Tholos* at Tivoli and the Temple of Concordia in the Forum. See Arnold Nesselrath, *Das Fossombroner Skizzenbuch*, London, The Warburg Institute, 1993, pp. 92-95 and fig. 10 (fol. 6v). Gardner, *The Roman Crucible*, p. 109.

39. Freeman, "A Fountain Basin by Drudus", pp. 123-125; Hesiod, *The Homeric Hymns and Homerica*, ed. Hugh Evelyn-White, Cambridge (MA), Harvard University Press, 1914, p. 136.

40. Roullet, *Egyptian and Egyptianizing Monuments*, p. 5, n. 1.

41. Albert Dessenne, *Le Sphinx Étude iconographique*, vol. I, *Des origins à la fin du second millénaire*, Paris, E. de Boccard, 1957, p. 106.

was also a royal symbol, and this association partially explains the widespread association of lions and sphinxes, an association often repeated in the Cosmati workshops. The difficult transition between a human head and leonine body was covered by the nemeses, a cloth covering that originally hid the ruler's hair. The pharaoh was always clean-shaven, whereas one of the Lateran sphinxes is majestically bearded. The Cosmati do not seem to have imitated female sphinxes, which existed in Egypt as representations of the female pharaoh Hatshepsut.[42] This omission may possibly be related to the largely Christian ecclesiastical locations of their imitations.

At Karnak and Luxor an avenue of sphinxes watched over the royal way, although normally in Egypt the sphinx appears to have been a cult image rather than a simple guardian.[43] Yet something of this tutelary function may run over into the Roman imitations. The paired sphinxes at the Lateran gaze inwards at the monastic community in the cloister walk. The later pair of smiling sphinxes set above the portal of the hospital church of S. Antonio near Santa Maria Maggiore retain this function of watching the outside world. They are among the latest of the Roman sphinxes completed by the executors or Cardinal Pietro Capocci († 1259) in the early 1260s (Fig. 34).[44] Capocci, cardinal-deacon of San Giorgio in Velabro, had served as legate in Germany and subsequently in central Italy during the papacy's exile at Lyons. Matthew Paris regarded him as a close and influential ally (*amicus prepotens*) of Innocent IV.[45] Neither of his executors are known to have had any contact with Egypt. Their choice of sphinxes was a Roman one, and such evidence as exists points to the role taken by Pietro Capocci himself.

The Capocci family were already significant patrons of the Cosmati workshops. Giovanni Giacomo Capocci, the cardinal's father, was responsible for one of the most important Cosmati monuments in Rome, the Capocci Tabernacle of 1256, once in the nave of the neighbouring basilica of Santa Maria Maggiore.[46]

42. *Ibid.*, pp. 103, 107.

43. Demisch, *Die Sphinx*, p. 57; Josef M. A. Janssen, "Review of Ursula Schweitzer, *Lőwe und Sphinx im alten Ägypten*, *(Ägyptologische Forschungen 15)*, Glückstadt, J.J. Augustin, 1949, *Bibliotheca Orientalis*, 6, 5, (Sept. 1949), pp. 133-136: 134, 136.

44. Gardner, *The Roman Crucible*, p. 113, n. 25 for the inscription. It reads: + DNS PETRUS CAPOC. CARD. MANDAVIT. COSTRVI. HOSPITALE ILOCO ISSTO. ET DNI O. TUSCUL. EPS. ET I. GAIETAN. CARD. EXECUTORES. ET FIEI FECERVT P AIA DNI PET CAPCC. (O(do) was Eudes de Châteauroux who became cardinal bishop of Tusculum in 1244, and Giangaetano Orsini (the later Nicholas III) who was made cardinal deacon of San Nicola in Carcere the same year. Paravicini Bagliani, *Cardinali di Curia*, pp. 198-209, 314-323. For Pietro Capocci, see Friedrich Reh, *Kardinal Peter Capocci Ein Staatsmann und Feldherr des XIII. Jahrhunderts*, Berlin, Dr. Emil Ebering, 1933, and Paravicini Bagliani, *Cardinali di Curia*, pp. 300-313. Pietro Capocci died 30 April 1259.

45. *Matthaei Parisiensis Monach Sancti Albani Chronica Majora*, vol. V, p. 79.

46. Talman Drawings, Vol. I, f. 96; Julian Gardner, "The Capocci Tabernacle in Santa Maria Maggiore", *Papers of the British School at Rome*, 25 (1970), pp. 220-234; Gardner, *Roman Crucible*, pp. 113-115; Claudia Bolgia, "The Felici Icon Tabernacle (1372) at S. Maria Aracoeli, Reconstructed: Lay Patronage, Sculpture and Marian Devotion in Trecento Rome", *Journal of the Warburg and Courtauld Institutes*, 68 (2005), pp. 27-72; Bolgia, *Reclaiming the Roman Capitol*, pp. 357-358.

Its original aspect is shown in a magnificent coloured drawing by John Talman, now in the collection of the Society of Antiquaries in London.[47] An exceptionally important example of lay patronage in 13th-century Rome, it was commissioned by the Senator Giacomo and his wife Vinia. Long dismantled, the dedicatory mosaic is now in the church of San Michele, at Vico in Lazio.[48] Three years later, the cardinal himself was to be buried in his newly built chapel of Santa Barbara in Santa Maria Maggiore. His preserved epitaph records his munificence as a patron.[49] His discriminating taste is confirmed by a notably elegant seal matrix.[50] A second substantial strand of evidence may be indicated by the dedication of the hospital church to Abbot Anthony.[51] Anthony was an Egyptian hermit whose cult was widespread in the Middle Ages and particularly associated with hospitals; he appears in the Roman Easter liturgy at San Saba in the 11th century, and his feast (17 January) was commemorated at both the Lateran and San Pietro.[52]

This location of sphinxes above the capital level is unique in medieval Rome and rare elsewhere.[53] At Sant'Antonio Abbate, they form part of an

47. Talman Drawings, Vol. I, f. 96; Gardner, "The Capocci Tabernacle", fig. XXXV.

48. Gardner, "The Capocci Tabernacle", fig. XXXIV. Gardner, *The Roman Crucible*, pp. 113-115.

49. Forcella, *Iscrizioni*, vol. IX, p. 10, no. 4; Reh, *Kardinal Peter Capocci*, p. 174. "Cardine praelatum genitum de stipite claro, / Quem rea mors rapuit, infima busta tenent. / Cultor iustitiae, rigidus servator honesti, / Quaeque dari voluit, pauca retenta tulit. / Gente Capocinus Petrus datus est sibi duplex / Ensis ab Ecclesia, quod tueatur eam. / Praetulit arma togae, Fredericum schismate plenum / Belli iure fugat, undique clarus ovat. / Donat opes largas, largo de pectore fusas / Gratis in hac aede Virgo Maria tibi. / Aurem vestit opus sculpit manus arte magistra / Mira columpna levat iste ministrat opes. / Condit opus sacra, condas animam precor huius / Aedibus aetheriis intemerata parens". ("A plain tomb encloses a celebrated cardinal of glorious family, stolen by cruel death. Champion of Justice, strenuous defender of honesty he cared little for possessions which he wished to give away. To Peter of the Capocci family the Church gave two swords for its safe guardianship. Girding the sword rather than the toga by right of war he put to flight Frederick, who was fomenting schism, and victorious everywhere, returned in triumph. He gave abundant gifts: thanks be given to the generous Virgin in this dwelling where gold embellishes the urn and a masterful hand works a splendid column; These support the wealth. The tomb encloses him and I, pure Virgin, pray that receive his soul in the heavenly dwelling"). An Italian translation is given in Guardo, *Titulus e Tumulus*, p. 42. The cult of Barbara was long-established in Rome and she appears in Santa Maria Antiqua in the 8th century. Reh, *Kardinal Peter Capocci*, pp. 168-169. She is present in the Sacramentary of Santa Maria Maggiore in the 12th century: Pierre Jounel, *Le culte des saints dans les basiliques du Latran et du Vatican au douzième siècle*, Rome, École Française de Rome, 1977, p. 319; Gardner, "The Capocci Tabernacle", pp. 220-234.

50. Julian Gardner, "Equestrian Saints and Cavalier Cardinals", in *Das Siegel als Medium der Kommunikation und des Transfers in europäischen Mittelalters*, ed. by Markus Späth and Andrea Stieldorf, Bonn 4 – 6 June 2019 (forthcoming).

51. For hospitals and the Antonite Order, see John Henderson, *The Renaissance Hospital*, New Haven/London, Yale University Press, 2006, pp. 17-18.

52. Jounel, *Le culte des saints*, pp. 214-215.

53. They occur at the Hohenstaufen castle at Prato and at Castel Maniace in Siracusa: Gardner, *The Roman Crucible*, p. 115, n. 30. There is a close-up photograph of the very weathered face in Gianandrea, "Creazioni à l'antique", p. 152, fig. 3.

elaborate splayed portal and constitute the only surviving façade sculpture in 13th-century Rome. They face frontally, couchant and smiling, and support attached columns on their backs. Despite their placement, their bodies are remarkably complete. Datable to around 1260, they are the last representatives of the vogue of Egyptianising sculpture in Rome itself. What is also noteworthy is that the Sant'Antonio portal appears to be the first of the Cosmati examples to make an overt link between sphinxes and Egypt.

The other late outlier, the sphinx by the Dominican sculptor Fra Paschalis at Viterbo, has a youthful face and a male lion's body (Fig. 35). Of all the surviving sphinxes in Rome and its neighbourhood, this one most accurately preserves the posture of its Egyptian original.[54] The radical turn of the head also indicates an assimilation of the model of the Nektanebo lion. The elaborate carved signature on the base occupies the place generally reserved for an inscription in hieroglyphics.[55] However, the ceremonially braided hair of the original Egyptian sphinx, which had been ignored by the earlier Cosmati workshops, assumes an extravagantly fashionable form here.[56] Two drawings, in the Royal Collection at Windsor and the Albertina at Vienna, show it standing before the tomb of the hereditary Roman Prefect Pietro da Vico in the Dominican church of Santa Maria in Gradi.[57] While, given the sculptor's affiliation, an original location in a Dominican church would be natural, there is little indication of its intended function. The highly polished body seems unsuited to supporting a candelabrum or other piece of church furniture.[58]

The sphinxes recreated by the Cosmati merit sustained attention, particularly in relation to their original Egyptian models, although they were more likely transmitted through ancient Roman imitations. We have some understanding of the process by

54. Roullet, *Egyptian and Egyptianizing Monuments*, p. 8, n. 8.

55. The inscription reads: + HOC OPUS · FECIT · FR'· PASCALIS · ROMAN' · ORD' · A ·D' · M' · C'C'· L· XXXUI.

56. I know of nothing strictly comparable in contemporary Italian sculpture; the coiffure of the female head from Frederick II's Capua Gate is considerably simpler. See Carl Willemsen, *Kaiser Friedrichs II. Triumphtor zu Capua*, Wiesbaden, Insel Verlag, 1953, Abb. 48, 49.

57. Windsor Codex Inv. No. 11906, and Albertina Italienische Architekturzeichnungen, Mappe 5, A 321. *Die mittelalterlichen Grabmäler in Rom und in Latium vom 13. bis 15. Jahrhundert. II, Abteilung, Quellen 5.Reihe I)*, vol. II, ed. by Jörg Garms, Andrea Sommerlechner and Werner Telesko, Vienna, Österreichischen Akademie der Wissenschaften, 1994, Abb. 271, 272; Claussen, *Magistri Doctissimi*, pp. 167-168, fig. 265. Claussen's ascription of the tomb of an unknown bishop lying in front of the tomb of Pope Clement IV (1268), *Magistri Doctissimi*, pp. 168-169 is unconvincing.

58. It is by no means certain that the sculptor is identical with the Paschalis who signed the base of the candelabrum in Santa Maria in Cosmedin. That is signed VIR PBVS ET DOCT PASCHALIS RITE VOCAT SVMO CVM STVDIO CODIDIT HVC CEREUM. The lack of Dominican affiliation and the self-praise argue against it being the same sculptor. The Dominican Fra Guglielmo, Nicola Pisano's assistant, a *conversus* of Santa Caterina at Pisa always indicated his Order. Paschalis is a not uncommon name in medieval Rome: Olof Brattö, *Nuovi studi di antroponimia fiorentina I nomi meno frequenti del Libro di Montaperti (An. MCCLX)*, ed. by Karl Michaëlsson, Stockholm, Almqvist & Wiksell, 1955, p. 175. Compare it to Gardner, *The Roman Crucible*, p. 144, n. 163.

which they came to the attention of Roman sculptural workshops. Equally, we can examine the internal chronology of the phenomenon from its beginnings early in the 13th century and demise in the last quarter. What has not been addressed is why ecclesiastical patrons and sculptors were keen to use the motif on church furniture and in cloister decoration. We must now turn to this problem.

There were, in fact, several members of the Sacred College with personal experience of Egypt for whom the imitation of Egyptian sculpture might have held an attraction, such as Pelayo († 1230), who was deeply involved in the Fifth Crusade and heavily responsible for the disastrous defeat at Mansura in August 1221.[59] Nicholas Mesarites had noted his arrogance upon entering Constantinople.[60] Oliver of Paderborn (†1227) and Jacques de Vitry (†1240) were the most important witnesses of the disintegration of the Egyptian campaign.[61] Oliver wrote an eloquent account of his experiences in the East, where he was active in the military campaigns.[62] In May 1218, Jacques was assigned by Honorius III as legate to the crusading forces at Damietta.[63]

These three cardinals – a Spaniard, a German and a Frenchman – were also longer-term residents at Rome, and they too must have observed and wondered at the pyramids and obelisks. Gerald, whose last recorded visit to Rome as a simple pilgrim was in 1206, would have seen the Egyptian statues in front of the

59. José M. Fernandez Catón, "El cardenal Leonés Pelayo Albanense 1206-1230", *Archivos Leoneses*, 7 (1953), pp. 99-113; Demetrio Mansilla, "El Cardenal hispano Pelayo Gaitán (1206-1230)", *Anthologica Annua*, 1 (1953), pp. 11-66; Maleczek, *Papst und Kardinalskolleg*, pp. 167-169; Werner Maleczek, "Zwischen lokaler Verankerung und universalem Horizont. Das Kardinalskollegium unter Innocenz III", in *Innocenzo III Urbis et Orbis*, vol. I, pp. 102-174: 154-156; James M. Powell, *Anatomy of a Crusade*, Philadelphia, University of Pennsylvania Press, 1986, pp. 188, 202; Pierre-Vincent Claverie, *Honorius III et l'Orient (1216-1227), Études et publication de sources inédites des Archives vaticanes (ASV)*, Leiden, Brill, 2013, pp. 46, 274.

60. August Heisenberg, *Neue Quellen zur Geschichte des lateinischen Kaisertums und der Kirchenunion III. Der Bericht Nikolaos Mesarites über die politischen und kirchlichen Ereignisse des Jahres 1214, Sitzungsberichte der Bayerischen Akademie de Wissenschaften Philosophisch-philologische und historische Klasse*, 3 Abhandlung, Munich, 1923. Maleczek, *Papst und Kardinalskolleg*, p. 167; Robert Figueira, "'Legatus apostolice Sedis': The Pope's 'Alter Ego' According to Thirteenth-Century Canon Law", *Studi Medievali*, 27 (1986), pp. 527-574: 569. Honorius III, on the other hand, saw him as the new Joshua: Christian Grasso, "Cardinale Pelagio d'Albano legato papale e predicatore della Quinta Crociata", *Revue d'Histoire Ecclésiastique*, 108 (2013), pp. 98-141: 107; Pressutti, *Regesta Honorii Papae III*, n. 2338: "*quasi alter Josue*".

61. Anna-Dorothee von den Brincken, "Islam und Oriens Christianus in den Schriften des Domscholasters Oliver († 1227)", in *Orientalische Kultur und Europäisches Mittelalter*, ed. by Albert Zimmermann, Ingrid Craemer-Ruegenberg and Gudrun Vuillemin-Diem, Berlin, De Gruyter, 1985, pp. 86-102. He was in Egypt 1217-1222.

62. Oliver of Paderborn, *Historia Damiatina*, ed. by Hermann Hoogeweg, *Die Schriften des Kölner Domscholasters, späteren Bischofs von Paderborn und Kardinal-Bischofs von S. Sabina Oliverus*, Tübingen, Litterarischer Verein in Stuttgart, 1894, pp. 159-280.

63. Maurice Coens, "Jacques de Vitry", *Biographie Nationale publiée par l'Académie Royale des Sciences, des Lettres et des Beaux-Arts de Belgie*, 31, Brussels, H. Thiry-van Buggenhoudt, 1962, cols. 402-475; von den Brincken, "Islam und Oriens Christianus", p. 89; Paravicini-Bagliani, *Cardinali di Curia*, p. 106.

Pantheon, and he too doubtless marvelled at the obelisks and pyramids of pagan Rome. Gervase, who visited in the second decade of the century, would probably have experienced much the same. Gregory, however, to whom we owe the most detailed reference to the statues outside the Pantheon, a church whose interior he personally paced out, could well have seen the cloister at the Lateran on his restlessly inquisitive sojourn in the city.

It may not, however, have been necessary to inspect the Egyptian pyramids *in situ*. Later in the century, Burchard of Mount Sion described them with some objectivity. Like Master Gregory looking at the pyramid of Cestius, he too dismissed the idea that they were granaries, preferring to regard them as tombs: "Horrea Joseph ibi vidi excelsa supra modum ita ut ad dietam et ad ½ miliare videantur. Incole vocant ea Horrea Ioseph, sed mihi videntur esse sepulcra sive tytuli sepulcrorum. Sunt enim pyramides tres in uno loco habentes ab angulo usque ad angulum 180 cubitos virilis stature et tante altitudinis quod nullo modo potest arcus usque ad summum iacere licet sed saepius attemptatum" ("There I saw Joseph's Granaries, which are exceedingly tall so as to be visible a day's journey and half a mile away. The inhabitants call them Joseph's Granaries, but they look to me like tombs or tomb-markers. For they are three pyramids in one place, from corner to corner measuring 180 cubits of a man's stature and so high that in no way can a bow shoot right to the top, as has quite often been tried").[64] These were monuments that cardinals like Jacques de Vitry and Oliver of Paderborn would have known about from personal experience.

Modern Egyptian artefacts were also available in 13th-century Rome. At the enthronement of Gregory IX in 1227, Egyptian figurated carpets were strewn on the floors of the Lateran palace.[65] But there were other, more pressing strategic and political reasons for the contemporary interest in Egypt. Primary among them was crusade: the Latins had finally realised that the road to Jerusalem lay through Egypt.[66] The catastrophic surrender at Damietta in 1221 was a recent wound. We should also remember that Francis of Assisi made an unsuccessful missionary journey to Egypt in 1219, despite attempts by Franciscan chroniclers to recast the episode as a victory.[67] Evidence of the encounter probably came from Francis' companion, Fra Illuminato. The Ayyubid Sultan al-Malik al-Kâmil gave Francis a

64. Rubin, "Burchard of Mount Sion's *Descriptio Terrae Sanctae*", p. 185. Burchard of Mount Sion, *Descriptio Terrae Sanctae*, p. 216.

65. *Le Liber Censuum de l'Église Romaine*, vol. II, p. 19 After arriving at Santa Maria Maggiore, Gregory IX rode to San Pietro (1227): "…Hinc cantica concrepant, inde preconia populi jubilante exsurgunt et per vicos singulos clamosum resonat Kyrieleison; aureis argentieisque platea distinguitur tapetis pictis ex Egypto prostrata, et tinctis Indie Gallieque coloribus ordinate composita, diversorum aromatum suavitate flagrabat". Agostino Paravicini Bagliani, *Il corpo del Papa*, Turin, Einaudi, 1994, p. 33.

66. Michael Chamberlain, "The Crusader Era and the Ayyubid Dynasty", in *Cambridge History of Egypt*, vol. I, *Islamic Egypt, 640 – 1517*, ed. by Carl F. Petry, Cambridge, Cambridge University Press, 1998, pp. 211-241: 222. John P. Cooper, *The Medieval Nile*, Cairo/New York, American University in Cairo Press, 2014, pp. 60, 150, 224-227, fig. A 1.19.

67. Leonhard Lemmens, "De sancto Francisco Christum praedicante coram sultan Aegypti", *Archivum Franciscanum Historicum*, 19 (1926), pp. 559-578. See also John Tolan,

patient hearing and despatched him gently homewards.[68] The first representation of the scene of Francis before the Sultan is, however, substantially later than our observers' Roman experience.[69]

Both the San Paolo and the Lateran cloisters have elaborately sculptured figural architraves facing into the central space. Again, this was a considerable luxury; it is absent from two other Benedictine cloisters built by Cosmati masons at San Lorenzo *fuori le mura* and at the great abbey of Sassovivo near Foligno.[70] The sculptured decoration of the Roman cloister architraves are indebted to other models, among them the classical theatre mask that caught Gervase of Tilbury's eye, set apotropaically into the gateway at Naples, perhaps alongside imperial portrait busts.[71] These are the nearest the Cosmati workshop got to portrait heads.

Giraldus and Gervase noted both pyramids and obelisks during their encounters with Rome in the first decade of the 13th century. If Gregory travelled to Rome in the 1230s, he might well have encountered such Egyptianising imagery. Whether or not he did so, its sudden vogue is probably explained by the emerging interest in Egypt provoked by preparations for the Fifth Crusade. The calamitous and humiliating outcome of the Christian invasion of Egypt would seem, equally, to have been good reason for the Egyptianising vogue to tail off rapidly. The sphinxes, which grimaced from choir enclosures at Cività Castellana and Ferentino and impassively watched the Lateran canons, might have come to appear as harbingers of ill fortune, not to be assumed automatically into the Roman sculptural imaginary of the 13th century. Furthermore, they were generally carved by sculptors like Drudus de Trivio, of limited technical accomplishment, and would have appeared lumpen and provincial in the face of the classical revival associated with the rapidly rising Hohenstaufen emperor Frederick II.[72]

Saint Francis and the Sultan: The Curious History of a Christian-Muslim Encounter, Oxford, Oxford University Press, 2009.

68. The episode appears first in Thomas of Celano, Vita I, 57 *Analecta Franciscana*, X, Quaracchi, Typographia Collegii S. Bonaventurae, 1926-1941, pp. 43-44; Hans L. Gottschalk, *Al-Malik al-Kāmil von Egypten und seine Zeit*, Wiesbaden, O. Harrassowitz, 1958; Rosalind Brooke, *The Image of Saint Francis*, Cambridge, Cambridge University Press, 2006, pp. 14, 44, 184.

69. The episode is first pictured on the Saint Francis panel now in the Bardi Chapel in Florence of c. 1263/1266. This date has been convincingly argued on iconographical grounds by Eamon Duffy, "Finding St Francis: Early Images, Early Lives", in *Medieval Theology and the Natural Body*, ed. by Peter Biller and Alistair Minnis, Woodbridge, York Medieval Press, 1997, pp. 193-236: 230.

70. Michele Faloci Pulignani, *I Marmorari Romani a Sassovivo presso Foligno*, Perugia, Unione Tip. cooperativa, 1915; Claussen, *Magistri doctissimi*, pp. 162-165.

71. See p. 67, note 73 above.

72. Arnold Esch, "Friedrich II. Und die Antike", in *Friedrich II. Tagung des Deutschen Historischen Instituts in Rom im Gedenkjahr 1994*, ed. by Arnold Esch and Norbert Kamp, *Bibliothek des Deutschen Historischen Institutes*, 85, Tübingen, Niemeyer, 1996, pp. 201-234.

7. Aftermaths: Beyond Rome

What, finally, did our visitors bring back with them from their shared Italian experience? Certainly financial indebtedness, as we know Thomas of Marlborough had to flee his creditors in Rome. In the case of Gerald, corrosive disappointment and a settled conviction that he had been betrayed. He had played his best cards in Rome and gained nothing. Gerald was to remain an archdeacon until his death. Of Gregory's financial circumstances, like so much else about him, we know nothing.

Gervase differed fundamentally from the others in that he was an Englishman who had made his career abroad. The others were all *en route*. After Otto IV's death and the death of his own wife, Gervase may have entered the Premonstratensian house of Notre-Dame de l'Huveaune in Marseilles.[1] Before that, his future depended on the fortunes of his feckless emperor; he, probably much less than the others, was in command of his own destiny. At Arles, with its prominent Roman ruins, he was perhaps the one of our four travellers most able to apply his experience to appreciate their importance and even their function. His official involvement with the sarcophagi still accessible at Les Alyscamps is well documented. Gregory, however, vanished from the scene as mysteriously as he had entered it.

In the case of Thomas, this marked an unexpected triumph over the odds. His Roman exploits established his status and contributed massively to his subsequent election as prior in 1218. To what extent did his Roman sojourn and his itineraries to and from the city affect him? The extensive refurbishment he undertook at Evesham Abbey is suggestive. As prior, he had restored the shrine of Saint Wystan and the high altar.[2] But his other additions are even more suggestive. Before the altar of Saint Peter, which is presumably the abbey's high altar, he erected a monumental crucifix and improved the existing illumination.[3] While this was not something Thomas was likely to have seen at Saint Peter's, or indeed anywhere

1. Gervase of Tilbury, *Otia Imperialia*, p. xxxvii.

2. "Et feretrum sancti Wistani nouum fecit, et tres tabulas maioris altaris reparauit": Thomas of Marlborough, *History of the Abbey of Evesham*, p. 488.

3. *Ibid.*, p. 496: "Et trabem ante altare sancti Petri cum cruce et ymaginibus reparauit et exaltauit ad maius luminare vestiarii".

else in early 13th-century Rome, it chimes with Innocent III's insistence that each altar was to have a crucifix on (or above) it. Gerald, we may also remember, had greatly praised the lighting within the Vatican basilica. Thomas' other action was to set up his own effigial tomb during his own lifetime, though he issued a modest disclaimer that it was for the reputation of Evesham Abbey.[4]

The use of marble for an effigial tomb at this date is unusual.[5] Tomb effigies were already erected in his immediate neighbourhood, most notably the tomb of King John at Worcester Cathedral, where there was also a precocious effigy of an early 13th-century bishop.[6] John's tomb, too, had been set between the shrines of Saint Oswald and Saint Dunstan.[7] Its vigorous effigy was carved from Purbeck marble. Whether the term "marble", which Thomas used in his *Chronicle*, at this date meant "Purbeck" is questionable, but there can be no certainty. As an effigial tomb for an abbot, it is precocious, and the setting is unusually prominent.[8] But a tomb effigy at this date would have been more likely encountered in England or France than in Rome, where the fashion was introduced only in the 1270s.[9] Desire for personal commemoration is perhaps more likely to have motivated Thomas of Marlborough. Commissioning a figural tomb during one's own lifetime foreshadows Boniface VIII.[10] Nevertheless, his repairs, embellishment and the provision of appropriate liturgical books for the high altar of the abbey is

4. *Ibid.*, p. 502: "Et sibi ipsi cum eisdem fecit mausoleum et incidit in lapide marmoreo superposito ymaginem episcopalem ad honorem ecclesie". Thomas died 12 September 1236.

5. It may be surmised that it was not actually marble, but highly polished Wenlock freestone. Abbot Adam (1161-1189) commissioned a splendid lectern for the abbey chapterhouse, which is probably the one now surviving in the dependent church of St Egwine, Norton (Worcs). Thomas of Marlborough, *History of the Abbey of Evesham*, p. 186. The stone and its place of origin is identified in Geoffrey Pearson, John Prentice, Alastair Pearson, "Three English Romanesque Lecterns", *The Antiquaries Journal*, 82 (2002), pp. 328-339: 329. As sacrist, Thomas had a new lectern made for the abbey choir: Thomas of Marlborough, *History of the Abbey of Evesham*, p. 488.

6. Frederick Crossley, *English Church Monuments*, London, B. T. Batsford, 1921, p. 188 (Worcester bishop). For John's tomb, see Paul Williamson, *Gothic Sculpture 1140-1300*, New Haven/London, Yale University Press, 1995, p. 111; Julian Gardner, "Likeness and/or Representation in French and English Royal Portraits c. 1250 – c. 1300", in *Das Porträt vor der Erfindung des Porträts*, ed. by Martin Büchsel and Peter Schmidt, Mainz, Philipp von Zabern, 2003, pp. 141-151: 142-143. John had died on 19 October and Cardinal Guala, as papal legate, was present at the Worcester for the coronation of his successor, the minor Henry III nine days later, but he could not have seen the royal effigy.

7. "...coram magni altari inter Sanctos Oswaldum et Wistanum": *Annales Prioratus de Wigornia A.D. 1 – 1377, Annales Monastici*, vol. IV, ed. by Henry R. Luard, London, Longmans, Green, Reader and Dyer, 1869, p. 407.

8. At Fountains Abbey, abbots were normally buried in the Chapterhouse. The first abbatial tomb in the church was in the middle of the 14th century. Roy Gilyard-Beer, "The Graves of the Abbots of Fountains", *The Yorkshire Archaeological Journal*, 59 (1987), pp. 45-50.

9. Julian Gardner, "Introduzione della tomba figurata in Italia centrale", in *L'Arte Gotica in Italia*, ed. by Valentino Pace and Martina Bagnoli, Naples, Electa, 1994, pp. 85-88, 207-220.

10. Julian Gardner, *The Tomb and the Tiara*, Oxford, Oxford University Press, 1992, pp. 107-109.

very much like Innocent III's programme of refurbishment of the sanctuary of the Vatican basilica.[11]

On the other hand, the classical sculptures of the type that so entranced Master Gregory in Rome could only have been visible in Winchester, where Henri de Blois apparently installed his booty. Classically inspired sculpture was certainly produced for Winchester Cathedral in the subsequent decades, and it may be that local sculptors inspected the bishop's statues.[12] None of our other three travellers had sufficient status or the means to emerge as a major artistic patron.

All told, however, the importance of our insular visitors to Rome is for the information they bring about curial procedures, and their current attitudes to the ancient past. Only Master Gregory made a serious attempt to understand what he saw in Rome and to form an aesthetic critique of ancient sculpture. There, the avid reception of classical sculpture and painting and its reutilisation most likely came from the contemporary craftsmen themselves. The sculptor of the sphinxes in the Lateran cloister evinced a greater awareness of the antique than the British visitors taken as a group. The fact that sphinxes and lions were employed not only in Rome, but in small towns in the city's immediate vicinity, strongly suggests that the impulse came from the sculptors rather than their patrons. It goes very much in step with the reception and exploitation of classical models visible contemporaneously in Lotharingia, the metal-working ateliers of the Meuse valley and the sculptural workshops of the cathedral façade at Reims.[13]

Finally, there is nothing in the observations and reflections of our travellers that suggests any shared intellectual affinity. Attempts to identify an English mentality or intellectual approach have not been conspicuously successful, and it is anachronistic in this context to attempt to define them.[14] Gerald and Gervase were members of the Anglo-Norman elite. Even during his expedition to Wales, Gerald preached at Haverfordwest, first in Latin and then in French.[15] Beyond

11. Thomas of Marlborough, *History of the Abbey of Evesham*, p. 494: "*Et textum maioris altaris sine libro reparauit*".

12. Williamson, *Gothic Sculpture*, p. 113 and fig. 173.

13. Samuele Vitali, "'*Sicut exploratoret spoliorum cupidus.*' Zu Methode und Funktion der Antiken-rezeption bei Nikolaus von Verdun", *Wiener Jahrbuch für Kunstgeschichte*, 52 (2002), pp. 9-46; Wilhelm Vöge, "Bahnbrecher des Naturstudiums um 1200", *Zeitschrift für bildende Kunst*, 24 (1914), pp. 193-216. Reprinted in *Bildhauer des Mittelalters. Gesammelte Studien von Wilhelm Vöge*, Berlin, Gebr. Mann, 1958, pp. 63-97. For an important recasting of the argument, see Willibald Sauerländer, "*Antiqui et Moderni* at Reims", *Gesta*, 42/1 (2003), pp. 19-37. The author's title is drawn from Map's *De nugis curialium*; Williamson, *Gothic Sculpture*, pp. 62-63.

14. Southern, *Robert Grosseteste*, pp. xxxiv-xxix, p. 322. See the review by Bruce Eastwood of Southern, *Robert Grosseteste*, original 1986 edition in *Speculum* 63/1 (1988), pp. 233-237.

15. *GC Opera*, vol. VI, bk I, ch. 11, p. 83; Gerald of Wales, *The Journey through Wales and Description of Wales*, p. 141. With typical hubris, he remarks that his eloquence was such that even those who could not understand either language were moved to take the Cross. *GC Opera*, vol. I, bk II, 18. Characteristically Gerald compares this action with St Bernard of Clairvaux preaching to the Germans: *GC Opera*, vol. I, p. 76: "*Simile contigit in Alemannia de beato Bernardo*".

their highly creditable Latin, it is uncertain to what extent either Thomas of Marlborough or Gregory used the vernacular. Like Gerald, Thomas was likely a product of the Parisian schools. Gerald's demonstrated capacity for minute observation of birds and works of art is an ability Master Gregory also shared, although he applied his visual perspicacity in quite a different way. Ancient Rome aroused his passionate curiosity, whereas Gerald earlier, an avid observer, was astonishingly constrained by Rome. His last farewell was that of a simple pilgrim. While Thomas skulked out at dawn, Gregory bade a lingering farewell to his goddess. Their departures were as dissimilar as their entrances.

Bibliography

Primary Sources

Adam of Eynsham, *Magna vita sancti Hugonis: The Life of St. Hugh of Lincoln*, ed. by Decima Douie and Hugh Farmer, London, Nelson, 1961-1962 (reprint Oxford, Oxford University Press, 1985)

Annales Prioratus de Wigornia A.D. 1 – 1377, Annales Monastici, vol. IV, ed. by Henry R. Luard, London, Longmans, Green, Reader and Dyer, 1869

Anonimo Romano, *Cronica*, ed. by Giuseppe Porta, critical edition, Milan, Adelphi, 1979

Burchard of Mount Sion, *Descriptio Terrae Sanctae*, ed. by John R. Bartlett, Oxford, Oxford University Press, 2019

Calendar of the Liberate Rolls Henry III, vol. I, *A.D. 1226-1240*, London, Longmans, Green, Reader and Dyer, 1916

Chronica Johannis de Oxenedes, ed. by Henry Ellis, London, Longman, Brown, Green, Longmans and Roberts, 1859

Cicero, *Oratio in Catilinam, I-IV*, transl. by Coll Macdonald, Cambridge, MA, Harvard University Press, 1977

Corpus Iuris Canonici, ed. by Emil Friedberg, Leipzig, Bernard Tauchnitz, 1881

Decretalium D. Gregorii Papae IX, Leipzig, Bernhard Tauchnitz, 1881, Lib. II, Titulus XXII, *De Fide Instrumentorum*

Desbonnets, Théodore, "Legenda Trium Sociorum, Édition critique", *Archivium Franciscanum Historicum*, 67 (1974), pp. 38-144

Die Schriften des Kölner Domscholasters, späteren Bischofs von Paderborn und Kardinal-Bischofs von S. Sabina Oliverus, ed. by Hermann Hoogeweg, Tübingen, Litterarischer Verein in Stuttgart, 1894

Geoffrey of Monmouth, *Historia Regum Britanniae*, ed. by Acton Griscom, London, Longmans, Green & Co., 1929

Gervase of Tilbury, *Otia Imperialia: Recreation for an Emperor*, ed. by Shelagh Banks and James Binns, Oxford, Oxford University Press, 2002

Gesta Pontificorum Romanorum, ed. by Philipp Jaffé and Samuel Löwenfeld, Leipzig, Veit, 1885-1888

Giraldi Cambrensis Opera, vol. I, *De rebus a se gestis*, ed. by John S. Brewer, London, Longman, Green, Longman and Roberts, 1861

Giraldi Cambrensis Opera, vol. II, *Gemma Ecclesiastica*, ed. by John S. Brewer, London, Longman, Green, Longman and Roberts, 1862

Giraldi Cambrensis Opera, vol. III, *De invectionibus, de jure et statu Menevensi ecclesiae*, ed. by John S. Brewer, London, Longman, Green, Longman and Roberts, 1863

Giraldi Cambrensis Opera, vol. IV, *Speculum ecclesiae*, ed. by John S. Brewer, London, Longman and Co., 1863

Giraldi Cambrensis Opera, vol. V, *Topographia Hibernica*, *Expugnatio Hibernica*, ed. by James Dimock, London, Longman, Green, Reader and Dyer, 1867

Giraldi Cambrensis Opera, vol. VI, *Itinerarium Kambriae, Descriptio Kambriae*, ed. by James Dimock, London, Longman, Green, Reader and Dyer, 1868

Giraldi Cambrensis Opera, vol. VII, *Vita S. Remigii, Vita S. Hugonis*, ed. by James Dimock, London, Longman and Co., 1877

Giraldi Cambrensis Opera, vol. VIII, *De principis instructione liber*, ed. by George Warner, London, Her Majesty's Stationery Office, 1891

Golubovich, Girolamo, *Biblioteca Bio-Bibliografica della Terra Santa e dell'Oriente Francescana*, vol. IV, Quaracchi, Typog. Franciscana, 1923, pp. 427-460

Gvillelmi Dvranti Rationale Divinorum Officiorvm, ed. by Anselme Davril and Timothy M. Thibodeau, Turnhout, Brepols, 1995-2000

Hagen, John J., *The Jewel of the Church: A Translation of* Gemma ecclesiastica *by Giraldus Cambrensis*, Leiden, Brill, 1979

Hampe, Karl, "Ein ungedruckter Bericht über das Konklave von 1241 im romischen römischen Septizonium", *Sitzungsberichte der Heidelberger Akademie der Wissenschaften Philosophisch-historische Klasse*, 4 (1913), pp. 1-34

Hesiod, *The Homeric Hymns and Homerica*, ed. by Hugh Evelyn-White, Cambridge (MA), Harvard University Press, 1914

Hildeberti Cenomannensis episcopi carmina minora, ed. by Brian A. Scott, Leipzig, Teubner, 1969

Hoade, Eugene, *Western Pilgrims: The Itineraries of Fr. Simon Fitzsimons (1322-23), a certain Englishman (1344-45), Thomas Byng (1392) and Notes on Other Authors and Pilgrims*, Jerusalem, Franciscan Press, 1952

Huillard-Breholles, Jean-Louis A., *Historia Diplomatica Friderici Secundi sive constitutiones, privilegia, mandata, instrumenta quae supersunt istius imperatoris et filiorum ejus. Accedunt epistolae paparum et documenta varia*, vol. V/2, Paris, Henri Plon, 1859, pp. 1077-1085

Itinerarium Symonis Semeonis ab Hybernia ad Terram Sanctam, *Scriptores Latini Hiberniae,* vol. IV, ed. by Mario Esposito, Dublin, Dublin Institute for Advanced Studies, 1960

Le Liber Censuum de l'Église Romaine, vol. II, ed. by Paul Fabre and Louis Duchesne, Paris, Fontemoing et Cie., 1910

Le Liber Pontificalis: Texte, introduction et commentaire, ed. by Louis Duchesne, Paris, Ernest Thorin, 1886-1892

Ludolf von Sudheim, *Ludolphi rectoris ecclesiae parochialis in Suchem de itinere Terra Sanctae liber*, ed. by Ferdinand Deycks, Stuttgart, Litterarischer verein, 1851

Magister Gregorius (XIIe *ou XIII*[e] *siècle), Narracio de Mirabilibus Romae*, ed. by Robert H. C. Huygens, Leiden, Brill, 1970

Master Gregorius: The Marvels of Rome, ed. and transl. by John Osborne, Toronto, Pontifical Institute of Medieval Studies, 1987.

Matthaei Parisiensis Monach Sancti Albani Chronica Majora, vol. V, ed. by Henry R. Luard, London, Longman & Co., 1880

Miedema, Nine Robintje, *Die "Mirabilia Romae". Untersuchungen ihre Überlieferung mit Edition der deutschen und niederländischen Texte*, Tübingen, Niemeyer, 1996

Nardella, Cristina, *Il fascino di Roma nel Medioevo: Le "Meraviglie di Roma" di maestro Gregorio*, Rome, Viella, 1997

Ovid, *The Art of Love and Other Poems*, transl. by John H. Mozley, rev. by George P. Goold, Cambridge (MA), Harvard University Press, 1979

Panvinio, Onofrio, *De praecipuis Urbis Romae sanctioribusque basilicis quas septem ecclesias vulgo vocant liber*, Rome 1570

Regesta Honorii Papae III iussu et munificentia Leonis XIII pontificis maximi ex Vaticanis archetypis aliisque fontibus edidit, ed. by Pietro Pressutti, Rome, Ex typ. Vaticana, 1888-1895

Rushforth, Gordon, "Magister Gregorius *de Mirabilibus Urbis Romae*: A New Description of Rome in the Twelfth Century", *Journal of Roman Studies*, 9 (1919), pp. 14-58

Rymer, Thomas, *Foedera, Conventiones, Literae et cujuscunque generis Acta Publica inter Reges Angliae et alios …*, London, George Eyre and Andrew Strachan, 1704-1735

Sicardi Cremonenses Episcopi Mitralis de Officiis, ed. by Gabor Sarbak and Lorenz Weinreich, Turnhout, Brepols, 2008 (Corpus Christianorum Continuatio Medievalis, 228)

Sinica Franciscana I Itinera et Relationes Fratrum Minorum saeculi XIII et XIV, ed. by Anastasius van den Wyngaert O.F.M., Florence, Quaracchi, 1929

Statius, *Silvae*, ed. by David R. Shackleton Bailey, Cambridge (MA), Harvard University Press, 2003

The Historia Pontificalis *of John of Salisbury*, ed. and transl. by Marjorie Chibnall, Oxford, Oxford University Press, 1986

The Historical Works of Gervase of Canterbury, vol. I, *The Chronicle of the Reigns of Stephen, Henry II, and Richard II*, ed. by William Stubbs, London, Longman & Co., 1879

The Journey through Wales and Description of Wales, ed. and transl. by Lewis Thorpe, Harmondsworth, Penguin Books, 1978

The Letters and Charters of Cardinal Guala Bicchieri, Papal Legate in England 1216-1218, ed. by Nicholas Vincent, Woodbridge, Boydell and Brewer, 1996

The Letters of John of Salisbury, vol. I, *The Early Letters (1153-1161)*, ed. by William J. Millor, Harold E. Butler and Christopher N. L. Brooke, Oxford, Oxford University Press, 1986

Thomas of Marlborough, *History of the Abbey of Evesham*, ed. by Jane E. Sayers and Leslie Watkiss, Oxford, Oxford University Press, 2003

Three Old English Elegies: The Wife's Lament, The Husband's Message, The Ruin, ed. by Roy F. Leslie, Manchester, Manchester University Press, 1961

Vacca, Flaminio, *Memorie di varie antichità trovate in diversi luoghi della città di Roma scritte ...nell'anno 1594*, in Flaminio Nardini, *Roma Antica*, 2nd ed., Rome, Ottavio Falconieri, 1704

Walter Map, *De Nugis Curialium: Courtiers' Trifles*, ed. and transl. by Montague R. James, rev. by Christopher N. L. Brooke and Roger A. B. Mynors, Oxford, Oxford University Press, 1983

Walteri Danielis Vita Ailredi Abbatis Revall, ed. by Frederick M. Powicke, London, Thomas Nelson and Sons, 1950

Willelmi Chronica Andrensis, in *Monumentae Germaniae Historica, Scriptores*, vol. XXIV, ed. by Johann Heller, Hanover, Hahnsche Buchhandlung, 1879 (reprint Stuttgart, Anton Hiersemann, 1964, pp. 684-773)

William of Andres, *The Chronicle of Andres*, ed. and transl. by Leah Shopkow, Washington, Catholic University Press, 2017

William of Malmesbury, *Gesta Regum anglorum*, ed. by Rodney Thomson and Michael Winterbottom, Oxford, Oxford University Press, 1998

Secondary Sources

Albanès, Joseph-Hyacinthe, *Gallia Christiana Novissima Histoire des Archevêchés, Évêchés et Abbayes de France, Arles*, 7 vols, Valence, Imprimerie Valentinoise, 1901

Anderson, James C., *Roman Architecture in Provence*, Cambridge, Cambridge University Press, 2013

Bacci, Michele, *Il pennello dell'Evangelista. Storia delle immagini sacre attribuite a san Luca*, Pisa, GISEM, 1998

Baldwin, John, *Masters, Princes and Merchants: The Social Views of Peter the Chanter and His Circle*, Princeton, Princeton University Press, 1970

Banks, Shelagh, "Tilbury, Gervase of", in *Dictionary of National Biography*, vol. LIV, Oxford, Oxford University Press, 2004, pp. 774–775

Barbiche, Bernard, "Les 'diplomates' pontificaux du moyen âge tardif à la première modernité", in *Offices et Papauté (XIVe-XVIIe siècle) Charges, Hommes, Destins*, ed. by Armand Jamme and Olivier Poncet, Rome, École Française de Rome, 2005

Barclay Lloyd, Joan, "The Architecture of the Medieval Monastery at S. Lorenzo fuori le mura, Rome", in *Architectural Studies in Memory of Richard Krautheimer*, ed. by Cecil L.Striker, Mainz, Philipp von Zabern, 1996, pp. 99-102

Bartlett, Robert, *Gerald of Wales: A Voice of the Middle Ages*, Stroud, History Press, 2006 (reprint 2013)

Bartlett, Robert, *Gerald of Wales and the Ethnographic Imagination*, Cambridge, Department of Anglo-Saxon, Norse and Celtic, 2013

Bartlett, Robert, "Gerald of Wales and the History of Llanthony Priory", *Gerald of Wales: New Perspectives on a Media Writer and Critic*, ed. by Georgia Henley and A. Joseph McMullen, Cardiff, University of Wales Press, 2018, pp. 81-93

Bartoloni, Gilda, *La lupa capitolina. Nuove prospettive di studio*, Rome, Bretschneider, 2010

Bate, A. Keith, "Walter Map and Giraldus Cambrensis", *Latomus*, 31 (1972), pp. 860-875

Bellini, Angelo, "L'Abbazia e la Chiesa di S. Donato in Sesto Calende", *Archivio Storico Lombardo*, 52 (1925), pp. 79-129

Bertelli, Carlo, *La Madonna di Santa Maria in Trastevere*, Rome, Eliograf, 1961

Biferali, Fabrizio, "Ridicula monstruositas? Spunti iconografici sul chiostro dei Vassalletto in San Paolo fuori le mura", *Arte Medievale*, 4 (2005), pp. 45-57

Bihrer, Andreas, "Selbstvergewisserung am Hof. Eine Interpretation von Walter Maps 'De nugis curialium' I 1-12", *Jahrbuch für internationale Germanistik*, 34 (2002), pp. 227-258

Binski, Paul, *Gothic Wonder*, London/New Haven, Yale University Press, 2014

Bird, Jessalyn, *Heresy, Crusade and Reform in the Circle of Peter the Chanter*, Ph.D Dissertation, Oxford University, 2001

Bolgia, Claudia, "The Felici Icon Tabernacle (1372) at S. Maria Aracoeli, Reconstructed: Lay Patronage, Sculpture and Marian Devotion in Trecento Rome", *Journal of the Warburg and Courtauld Institutes*, 68 (2005), pp. 27-72

Bolgia, Claudia, *Reclaiming the Roman Capitol: S. Maria in Aracoeli from the Altar of Augustus to the Franciscans c. 500-1450*, London, Routledge, 2017

Bolgia, Claudia, Rosamond McKitterick, John Osborne, eds, *Rome across Time and Space: Cultural Transmission and the Exchange of Ideas, c. 500-1400*, Cambridge, Cambridge University Press, 2011

Bolton, Brenda, "A New Rome in a Small Place? Imitation and Re-Creation in the Patrimony of St Peter", in *Rome across Time and Space: Cultural Transmission and the Exchange of Ideas, c. 500-1400*, ed. by Claudia Bolgia, Rosamond McKitterick and John Osborne, Cambridge, Cambridge University Press, 2011, pp. 305-322

Bombi, Barbara, "Petitioning Between England and Avignon in the First Half of the Fourteenth Century", in *Medieval Petitions: Grace and Grievance*, ed. by W. Mark Ormerod, Gwilym Dodd and Anthony Musson, Woodbridge, York Medieval Press, 2009, pp. 64-81

Bony, Jean, *French Gothic Architecture of the 12th and 13th Centuries*, Berkeley, University of California Press, 1983

Boschung, Dietrich, "Die *narracio de mirabilibus urbis Romae* des magister Gregorius", in *Wunder Roms im Blick des Nordens von der Antike bis zur Gegenwart*, ed. by Cristoph Stiegemann, Petersberg, Michael Imhof, 2017, pp. 76-89

Bosman, Lex, "Constantine's Spolia: A Set of Columns for San Giovanni in Laterano and the Arch of Constantine in Rome", in *The Basilica of Saint John Lateran to 1600*, ed. by Lex Bosman, Ian Haynes and Paolo Liverani, Cambridge, Cambridge University Press, 2020, pp. 168-196

Boureau, Alain, "How Law Came to the Monks: The Use of Law in English Society at the Beginning of the Thirteenth Century", *Past and Present*, 167 (2000), pp. 29-74

Brattö, Olof, *Nuovi studi di antroponimia fiorentina. I nomi meno frequenti del Libro di Montaperti (An. MCCLX)*, ed. by Karl Michaëlsson, Stockholm, Almqvist & Wiksell, 1955 (Romanica Gothoburgensia, 1).

Brattö, Olof, *Studi di antroponimia fiorentina. Il Libro di Montaperti (An. MCCLX)*, Göteborg, Elanders Boktrykerei, 1953

Brentano, Robert, *Rome before Avignon*, New York, Basic Books, 1974

Brentano, Robert, *Two Churches: England and Italy in the Thirteenth Century*, Princeton, Princeton University Press, 1968

Brooke, Rosalind, *The Image of St Francis*, Cambridge, Cambridge University Press, 2006

Buddensieg, Tilmann, "Criticism and Praise of the Pantheon in the Middle Ages and Renaissance", in *Classical Influences on European Culture A.D. 500-1500*, ed. by Robert R. Bolgar, Cambridge, Cambridge University Press, 1971, pp. 259-267

Burstyn, Shai, "Is Gerald of Wales a Credible Musical Witness?" *The Musical Quarterly*, 72/2 (1986), pp. 155-169

Calabi Limentani, Ida, "Sul non saper leggere le epigrafi classiche nei secoli XII e XIII: sulla scoperta graduale delle abbreviazioni", *Acme*, 23 (1970), pp. 253-282

Camille, Michael, *The Gothic Idol: Ideology and Image-Making in Medieval Art*, Cambridge, Cambridge University Press, 1989

Campanelli, Maurizio, "Monuments and Histories: Ideas and Images of Antiquity in Some Descriptions of Rome", in *Rome across Time and Space: Cultural Transmission and the Exchange of Ideas, c. 500-1400*, ed. by Claudia Bolgia, Rosamond McKitterick and John Osborne, Cambridge, Cambridge University Press, 2011, pp. 35-51

Carocci, Sandro, "Mobilità papale e territorio: problemi di metodo e di interpretazione", in *Itineranza pontificia: mobilità della curia papale nel Lazio (secoli XII-XIII)*, ed. by Sandro Carocci, Rome, Istituto storico italiano per il medioevo, 2003, pp. 81-100

Carruba, Anna M., *La lupa capitolina*, Rome, Bretschneider, 2006

Carruthers, Mary, *The Experience of Beauty in the Middle Ages*, Oxford, Oxford University Press, 2013

Chamberlain, Michael, "The Crusader Era and the Ayyubid Dynasty", in *Cambridge History of Egypt*, vol. I, *Islamic Egypt, 640-1517*, ed. by Carl F. Petry, Cambridge, Cambridge University Press, 1998, pp. 211-241

Cheney, Christopher, "King John and the Papal Interdict", *Bulletin of the John Rylands Library*, 31 (1948), pp. 295-317

Cheney, Christopher, "John of Ferentino, Papal Legate in England", *English Historical Review*, 76 (1961), pp. 654-656

Cheney, Christopher, *Pope Innocent III and England*, Stuttgart, Hiersemann, 1976

Cheney, Mary G., "Mauger", in *Dictionary of National Biography*, vol. XXXVII, Oxford, Oxford University Press, 2004, pp. 414-415

Clarke, Peter D., *The Interdict in the Thirteenth Century*, Oxford, Oxford University Press, 2007

Claussen, Peter Cornelius, *Chartres-Studien Zu Vorgeschichte, Funktion und Skulptur der Vorhallen*, Wiesbaden, Franz Steiner Verlag, 1975

Claussen, Peter Cornelius, *Magistri doctissimi Romani die romischen Marmorkunstler des Mittelalters*, Stuttgart, Franz Steiner Verlag, 1987

Claussen, Peter Cornelius, "Scultura romana al tempo di Federico II", in *Federico II e l'Arte del Duecento italiano, Atti della III Settimana di Studi di Storia dell'Arte Medievale dell'Università di Roma (15-20 Maggio 1978)*, ed. by Angiola Maria Romanini, Galatina, 1980, vol. I, pp. 325-338

Claussen, Peter Cornelius, Daniela Mondini, Darko Senekovic, *Die Kirchen der Stadt Rom im Mittelalter 1050 – 1300*, Bd. 3 G-L, Stuttgart, Franz Steiner Verlag, 2010

Claverie, Pierre-Vincent, *Honorius III et l'Orient (1216-1227). Études et publication de sources inédites des Archives vaticanes (ASV)*, Leiden, Brill, 2013

Coens, Maurice, "Jacques de Vitry", *Biographie Nationale publiée par l'Académie Royale des Sciences, des Lettres et des Beaux-Arts de Belgie*, vol. XXXI, Brussels, H. Thiry-van Buggenhoudt, 1962

Coldstream, Nicola, "English Decorated Shrine Bases", *Journal of the British Archaeological Association*, 39/1 (1976), pp. 15-34

Coleman, Edward, "Sicard of Cremona as Legate of Innocent III in Lombardy", in *Innocenzo III Urbis et Orbis. Atti del Congresso Internazionale Roma, 9-15 settembre 1998*, vol. II, ed. by Andrea Sommerlechner, Rome, 2003, pp. 929-953

Cooper, John P., *The Medieval Nile*, Cairo/New York, American University in Cairo Press, 2014

Corso, Antonio, "L'Afrodite Capitolina e l'arte del Cefisodoto il giovane", *Quaderni ticinesi di numismatica e antichità classiche*, 21 (1992), pp. 131-157

Corso, Antonio, *The Art of Praxiteles II: The Mature Years*, Rome, Bretschneider, 2007

Courtenay, William J., "The Academic and Intellectual Worlds of Ockham", in *The Cambridge Companion to Ockham*, ed. by Paul Vincent Spade, Cambridge, Cambridge University Press, 1999, pp. 17-30

Courtenay, William J., "Theology and Theologians from Ockham to Wyclif", in *The History of the University of Oxford*, vol. II, ed. by Jeremy I. Catto and Ralph Evans, Oxford, Oxford University Press, 1992, pp. 1-34

Crossley, Frederick, *English Church Monuments*, London, B. T. Batsford, 1921

Curran, Brian, *The Egyptian Renaissance: The Afterlife of Ancient Egypt in Early Modern Italy*, Chicago, University of Chicago Press, 2007

Curtius, Ernst R., *European Literature and the Latin Middle Ages*, London, Routledge, 1953

da Bra, Giuseppe, *Le iscrizioni latine di S. Lorenzo fuori le mura*, Rome, Scuola Tipografica Pio X, 1931

Davenport, Tony, "Sex, Ghosts and Dreams: Walter Map (1135? – 1210?) and Gerald of Wales (1146-1223)", in *Writers of the Reign of Henry II: Twelve Essays*, ed. by Ruth Kennedy and Simon Meecham-Jones, New York, Palgrave, 2006, pp. 133-150

De Strobel, Anna Maria, Nicoletta Bernacchio, "The Medieval Portico of Saint John Lateran", in *The Basilica of Saint John Lateran to 1600*, ed. by Lex Bosman, Ian Haynes and Paolo Liverani, Cambridge, Cambridge University Press, 2020, pp. 276-293

Deér, Josef, *The Dynastic Porphyry Tombs of the Norman Period in Sicily*, Cambridge (MA), Harvard University Press, 1959

Deimling, Barbara, "Das mittelalterliche Kirchenportal in seiner rechtsgeschichtliche Bedeutung", in *Romanik*, ed. by Rolf Toman, Cologne, Feierabend, 1996

Demisch, Heinz, *Die Sphinx Geschichte ihrer Darstellung von den Anfängen bis zur Gegenwart*, Stuttgart, Urachhaus, 1977

Demus, Otto, *The Mosaics of San Marco*, Chicago, University of Chicago Press, 1988

Dessenne, Albert, *Le Sphinx Étude iconographique*, vol. I, *Des origins à la fin du second millénaire*, Paris, E. de Boccard, 1957

Die römische Kurie und das Geld. Von der Mitte des 12. Jahrhunderts bis zum frühen 14. Jahrhundert, ed. by Werner Maleczek, Ostfildern, J. Thorbeke, 2018, pp. 118-124

Dinzelbacher, Peter, *Structures and Origins of the Twelfth-Century "Renaissance"*, Stuttgart, Anton Hiersemann, 2017

Dotti, Ugo, *Le familiari*, vol. III, Rome, Archivio Guido Izzo, 1994

Duchesne, Louis, "Le nom d'Anaclet II au palais de Latran", *Mélanges d'Archéologie et d'Histoire*, 9 (1889), pp. 355-362

Duffy, Eamon, "Finding St Francis: Early Images, Early Lives", in *Medieval Theology and the Natural Body*, ed. by Peter Biller and Alistair Minnis, Woodbridge, York Medieval Press, 1997, pp. 193-236

Dulière, Cécile, *Lupa romana. Études de philology, d'archéologie et d'histoire anciennes, 17*, Rome, Institut Historique Belge de Rome, 1979

Dunbabin, Jean, "Careers and Vocations", in *The History of the University of Oxford*, vol. I, ed. by Jeremy I. Catto, Oxford, Oxford University Press, 1984, pp. 565-605

Duprat, Eugène, "Histoire des Légendes Saintes de Provence", *Mémoires de l'Institut Historique de Provence*, 17 (1940), pp. 118-198; 18 (1941), pp. 87-186

Dykmans, Marc, "Le cardinal Annibal de Ceccano (vers 1282-1350), étude biographique et testament du 17 juin 1348", *Bulletin de l'Institut Historique Belge de Rome*, 43 (1973), pp. 145-344

Eastwood, Bruce, "Review of Richard Southern, *Robert Grosseteste: The Growth of an English Mind in Mediaeval Europe*, Oxford, 1986", *Speculum*, 63/1 (1988), pp. 233-237

Egger, Hermann, *Römische Veduten*, vol. II, Vienna, Anton Schroll, 1931

Ein Weltbild vor Columbus. Die Ebstorfer Weltkarte. Interdiziplinäres Kolloquium, ed. by Hartmut Kugler and Eckhard Michael, Weinheim, VCH Acta Humaniora, 1988

Esch, Arnold, "Friedrich II. und die Antike", in *Friedrich II. Tagung des Deutschen Historischen Instituts in Rom im Gedenkjahr 1994, Bibliothek des Deutschen Historischen Institutes, 85*, ed. by Arnold Esch and Norbert Kamp, Tübingen, Niemeyer, 1996, pp. 201-234

Evans, H. Wyn, "The Bishops of St. Davids from Bernard to Bec", in *Medieval Pembrokeshire*, ed. by Ronald F. Walker, Haverfordwest, Pembrokeshire Historical Society, 2002, pp. 279-311

Fedele, Pietro, "L'iscrizione del Chiostro di San Paolo", *Archivio della R. Società Romana di Storia Patria*, 44 (1921), pp. 279-276

Fernandez Catón, José M., "El cardenal Leonés Pelayo Albanense 1206-1230", *Archivos Leoneses*, 7 (1953), pp. 99-113

Figueira, Robert, "'Legatus apostolice Sedis': The Pope's 'Alter Ego' According to Thirteenth-Century Canon Law", *Studi Medievali*, 27 (1986), pp. 527-574

Fonnesberg-Schmidt, Iben, William Kynan Wilson, "Smiling, Laughing, and Joking at Rome: Thomas of Marlborough and Gerald of Wales at the Court of Innocent III", *Papers of the British School at Rome*, 86 (2018), pp. 153-181

Forcella, Vincenzo, *Iscrizioni delle chiese e di altri edifici di Roma dal secolo XI fino ai giorni nostri*, 14 vols, Rome, Tipografia delle scienze matematiche e fisiche, 1869-1884

Freeman, Elizabeth, "A Fountain Basin by Drudus de Trivio (fl c 1230 – 40): A Reconsideration", *Antiquaries Journal*, 99 (2019), pp. 105-132

Galieti, Alberto, "Memorie della chiesa medievale di Cività Lavinia", *L'Arte*, 12 (1909), pp. 349-358

Galland, Bruno, "Les hommes de la culture dans la diplomatie pontificale au XIIIe siècle", *Mélanges de l'École Française de Rome Moyen Age*, 108 (1996), pp. 615-643

Gans, Henning, "Der Widder von Kastell Maniace. Eine Bronze atoninischer Zeit?" *Antike Kunst*, 48 (2005), pp. 73-99

Gardner, Julian, "An Introduction to the Iconography of the Medieval Italian City Gate", *Dumbarton Oaks Papers*, 41 (1988), pp. 199-213

Gardner, Julian, "Equestrian Saints and Cavalier Cardinals", in *Das Siegel als Medium der Kommunikation und des Transfers in europäischen Mittelalters*, ed. by Markus Späth and Andrea Stieldorf, Bonn (forthcoming)

Gardner, Julian, "Introduzione della tomba figurata in Italia centrale", in *L'Arte Gotica in Italia*, ed. by Valentino Pace and Martina Bagnoli, Naples, Electa, 1994, pp. 85-88, 207-220

Gardner, Julian, "L'architettura del *Sancta Sanctorum*", *Sancta Sanctorum*, ed. by Carlo Pietrangeli, Milan, Electa, 1995, pp. 19-38

Gardner, Julian, "Likeness and/or Representation in French and English Royal Portraits c. 1250 – c. 1300", in *Das Porträt vor der Erfindung des Porträts*, ed. by Martin Büchsel and Peter Schmidt, Mainz, Philipp von Zabern, 2003, pp. 141-151

Gardner, Julian, "The Capocci Tabernacle in Santa Maria Maggiore", *Papers of the British School at Rome*, 25 (1970), pp. 220-234

Gardner, Julian, "The Cardinals' Music: Musical Interests at the Papal Curia c. 1200-c. 1304", *Early Music History*, 34 (2015), pp. 97-132

Gardner, Julian, *The Roman Crucible: The Artistic Patronage of the Papacy 1198-1304*, Munich, Hirmer Verlag, 2013

Gardner, Julian, "Thirteenth-Century Gothic Façades in Italy", in *Medioevo: arte e storia, Atti del Convegno internazionale di studi, Parma 18-22 settembre 2007*, ed. by Arturo Carlo Quintavalle, Milan, 2008, pp. 669-680

Gardner, Julian, *The Tomb and the Tiara*, Oxford, Oxford University Press, 1992

Garms, Jörg, et al., *Die mittelalterlichen Grabmäler in Rom und Latium von 13. bis 15. Jahrhundert. I. Die Grabplatten und Tafeln*, Rome/Vienna, Verlag der Österreichischen Akademie der Wissenschaften, 1981 (Publikationen de Österreichischen Kulturinstituts in Rom, II, Abteilung, Quellen 5. Reihe I)

Garms, Jörg, Andrea Sommerlechner, Werner Telesko, *Die mittelalterlichen Grabmäler in Rom und in Latium vom 13. bis 15. Jahrhundert. II, Die Monumentalgräber*, Vienna, Österreichischen Akademie der Wissenschaften, 1994 (Publikationen de Österreichischen Kulturinstituts in Rom, II, Abteilung, Quellen 5. Reihe I)

Gauvain, Alexis, "La Colonna Santa Museo Storico Artistico del Tesoro di San Pietro", *Archivum Sancti Petri Bollettino d'Archivio*, 28-29, Città del Vaticano, Edizioni Capitolo Vaticano, 2015

George, Wilma, Brunsdon Yapp, *The Naming of the Beasts*, London, Duckworth, 1991

Gerald of Wales: New Perspectives on a Medieval Writer and Critic, ed. by Georgia Henley and Joseph Mullen, Cardiff, University of Wales Press, 2018

Gianandrea, Manuela, "Creazioni à l'antique. I Vassalletto e il fascino della sfinge egizia nel medioevo romano", *Hortus Artium Medievalium*, 16 (2010), pp. 151-160

Gianandrea, Manuela, "Drudo di Trivio e Luca di Cosma gli artisti le opere e il loro intervento a Civita Castellana", in *La cattedrale cosmatesca di Civita Castellana, Atti del Convegno internazionale di studi (Civita Castellana 2010)*, ed. by Luca Creti, Rome, Bretschneider, 2012, pp. 217-232

Gianandrea, Manuela, *La scena del sacro. L'arredo liturgico nel basso Lazio tra XI e XIV secolo*, Rome, Viella, 2006

Gianandrea, Manuela, "L'Egitto dei faraoni nella Roma dei papi: riflessioni sull'Egitto nella cultura medievale tra storia, religione e mito", in *La Lupa e le sfinge: Roma e l'Egitto dalla storia al mito, Mostra, Roma 2008*, ed. by Eugenio Lo Sardo, Milan, Electa, 2008, pp. 132-142

Gibson, Bruce, "Hildebert of Lavardin on the Monuments of Rome", in *Word and Context in Latin Poetry: Studies in Memory of David West*, ed. by Anthony Woodman and Jaap Wisse, Cambridge, Cambridge University Press, 2017, pp. 131-154

Gilyard-Beer, Roy, "The Graves of the Abbots of Fountains", *The Yorkshire Archaeological Journal*, 59 (1987), pp. 45-50

Giovannoni, Gustavo, "Opere dei Vassalletti marmorari romani", *L'Arte*, 11 (1908), pp. 262-283

Giovenale, Giovanni B., "Il chiostro medievale di San Paolo fuori le mura", *Bullettino della Commissione Archeologica Comunale di Roma*, 45 (1917), pp. 125-167

Given-Wilson, Christopher, *The Chronicle of Adam Usk 1377-1421*, Oxford, Oxford University Press, 1997

Gottschalk, Hans L., *Al-Malik al-Kāmil von Egypten und seine Zeit*, Wiesbaden, O. Harrassowitz, 1958

Gransden, Antonia, *Historical Writing in England*, 2 vols, London, Routledge, 1994

Gransden, Antonia, "Realistic Observation in Twelfth-Century England", *Speculum*, 47 (1972), pp. 29-51

Guardo, Marco, "Epitafi di Papi Cardinali ed alti dignitari della Curia Pontificia tematiche e stile nell'epigrafia poetica del XIII secolo", *Archivio della Società Romana di Storia Patria*, 122 (1999), pp. 125-134

Guardo, Marco, *Titulus e tumulus*, Rome, Viella, 2008

Halliwell, Stephen, "The Function and Aesthetics of the Greek Tragic Mask", in *Intertextualiät in der griechisch-römischen Komödie*, ed. by Niall Slater and Bernhard Zimmermann, Stuttgart, M&P Verlag, 1993, pp. 195-211

Hammond, Nicholas, Michael Everett, *Birds of Britain and Europe*, London, Pan Books, 1980

Harvey, Paul D. A., *Mappa Mundi: The Hereford World Map*, Hereford, Hereford Cathedral, 2001

Haskell, Francis, Nicholas Penny, *Taste and the Antique: The Lure of Classical Sculpture 1500-1900*, New Haven/London, Yale University Press, 1981

Heijmans, Marc, *Arles durant l'Antiquité tardive de la Duplex Arelas à l'urbs Genesii*, Rome, École Française de Rome, 2004, pp. 139-160

Heisenberg, August, *Neue Quellen zur Geschichte des lateinischen Kaisertums und der Kirchenunion III. Der Bericht Nikolaos Mesarites über die politischen und kirchlichen Ereignisse des Jahres 1214, Sitzungsberichte der Bayerischen Akademie de Wissenschaften Pilosophisch-philologische und historische Klasse*, Jg.1923, 3 Abhandlung, Munich, 1923

Henderson, George, *From Durrow to Kells*, London, Thames and Hudson, 1987

Henderson, John, *The Renaissance Hospital*, New Haven/London, Yale University Press, 2006

Herde, Peter, *Audientia Litterarum Contradictarum Untersuchungen über die päpstlichen Justizbreve und die päpstliche Delegationsgerichtsarkeit vom 13. bis zum Beginn des 16. Jahrhunderts*, Tübingen, Niemeyer, 1970

Herklotz, Ingo, "Der Campus Lateranensis im Mittelalter", *Römisches Jahrbuch*, 22 (1985), pp. 1-43

Herklotz, Ingo, "Der mittelalterliche Fassadenportikus der Lateranbasilika und seine Mosaiken, Kunst und Propaganda am Ende des 12. Jahrhunderts", *Römisches Jahrbuch der Bibliotheca Hertziana*, 25 (1989), pp. 25-95

Herklotz, Ingo, "Die Beratungsräume Calixtus' II im Lateranpalast und ihre Fresken. Kunst und Propaganda am Ende des Investiturstreits", *Zeitschrift für Kunstgeschichte*, 52 (1989), pp. 145-214

Herklotz, Ingo, *Gli eredi di Costantino. Il papato, il Laterano e la propaganda visive nel XII secolo*, Rome, Viella, 2000

Higgins, Colin, Kat. n. 51, *Narracio de Mirabilibus Urbis*, Cambridge, St. Catherine's College MS 3 (E.4.96), in *Wunder Roms im Blick des Nordens von der Antike bis zur Gegenwart*, ed. by Christoph Stiegmann, Imhof Peterberg, 2017, pp. 358-360

Hohler, Christopher, "A Note on Jacobus", *Journal of the Warburg and Courtauld Institutes*, 35 (1972), pp. 31-80

Holdsworth, Christopher, "Langton, Stephen (c. 1150-1228)", in *Dictionary of National Biography*, vol. XXXII, Oxford, Oxford University Press, 2004, pp. 516-521

Holmes, Urban, "Gerald the Naturalist", *Speculum*, 11 (1936), pp. 110-121

Howlett, David R., "Two Old English Encomia", *English Studies*, 57 (1976), pp. 289-293

Hyde, Kenneth, "Medieval Descriptions of Cities", *Bulletin of the John Rylands Library*, 48/2 (1968), pp. 308-344

Iacobini, Antonio, "Le arti del metallo: oreficeria e bronzi", in *Roma nel Duecento. L'arte nella città dei papi dall'Innocenzo III a Bonifacio VIII*, ed. by Angiola Maria Romanini, Turin, Ed. Seat, 1991, pp. 306-319

Il portico medievale di San Giovanni in Laterano: I frammenti ritrovati, ed. by Anna Maria De Strobel, Città del Vaticano, Edizioni Musei Vaticani, 2019

Internullo, Dario, "Decus Urbis. Un'altra prospettiva sui Mirabilia di Roma e le origini del decoro urbano (secoli XII-XV)", *Quaderni Storici*, 1 (2020), pp. 159-183

Iversen, Erik, *Obelisks in Exile*, vol. I, *The Obelisks of Rome*, Copenhagen, Gad, 1968

Jäggi, Carola, "*Mater et Caput Omnium Ecclesiarum*: Visual Strategies in the Rivalry Between San Giovanni in Laterano and San Pietro in Vaticano", in *The Basilica of Saint John Lateran to 1600*, ed. by Lex Bosman, Ian Haynes and Paolo Liverani, Cambridge, Cambridge University Press, 2020, pp. 294-317

James, Montague Rhodes, *A Descriptive Catalogue of the Manuscripts in the Library of St. Catherine's College, Cambridge*, Cambridge, Cambridge University Press, 1925

Janssen, Josef M. A., "Review of Ursula Schweitzer, *Lőwe und Sphinx im alten Ägypten, (Ägyptologische Forschungen 15)*, Glückstadt, J.J. Augustin, 1949", *Bibliotheca Orientalis*, 6/5 (Sept. 1949), pp. 133-136

Jounel, Pierre, *Le culte des saints dans les basiliques du Latran et du Vatican au douzième siécle*, Rome, École Française de Rome, 1977

Kajanto, Iiro, *Classical and Christian Studies in the Latin Epitaphs of Medieval and Renaissance Rome*, Helsinki, Suomalainen Tiedeakatemia, 1980

Kay, Richard, "Gerald of Wales and the Fourth Lateran Council", *Viator*, 29 (1988), pp. 79-93

Kenyon, John, "Manorbier Castle", *The Archaeological Journal*, 167 (2010), pp. 43-45

Kessler, Herbert, "Christ's Dazzling Dark Face", in *Intorno al Sacro Volto. Genova, Bisanzio e il Mediterraneo (XI-XVI secolo)*, ed. by Anna Rosa Calderoni Masetti, Colette Dufour Bozzo and Gerhard Wolf, Venice, Marsilio, 2007, pp. 231-246

Kinney, Dale, "Fact and Fiction in the *Mirabilia Urbis Romae*", in *Roma Felix: Formation and Reflections of Medieval Rome*, ed. by Éamonn Ó. Carragain and Carol Neuman de Vegvar, Aldershot, Ashgate, 2007, pp. 235-252

Kinney, Dale, "The Horse, the King and the Cuckoo: Medieval Narrations of the Statue of Marcus Aurelius", *Word and Image*, 18 (2002), pp. 372-398

Kinney, Dale, "*Mirabilia Urbis Romae*", in *The Classics in the Middle Ages*, ed. by Aldo Bernardo and Saul Levin, Binghampton (NY), Center for Medieval and Early Renaissance Studies, 1990, pp. 207-221

Kinney, Dale, "Rome in the Twelfth Century: *Urbs fracta* and *renovation*", *Gesta*, 45/2 (2006), pp. 199-220

Kitzinger, Ernst, "A Virgin's Face: Antiquarianism in Twelfth-Century Art", *Art Bulletin*, 62 (1980), pp. 6-19

Kitzinger, Ernst, "The Arts as Aspects of a Renaissance Rome and Italy", in *Renaissance and Renewal in the Twelfth Century*, ed. by Robert L. Benson and Giles Constable, Oxford, Oxford University Press, 1982, pp. 637-670

Kleefisch-Jobst, Ursula, *Santa Maria sopra Minerva: Ein Beitrag zur Architektur der Bettelorden in Mittelitalien*, Münster, Nodus Publikationen, 1991

Kleiner, Diana, "The Study of Roman Triumphal and Honorary Arches 50 Years After Kähler", *Journal of Roman Archaeology*, 2 (1989), pp. 195-206

Krautheimer, Richard, *Rome: Profile of a City*, Princeton, Princeton University Press, 1980

Krautheimer, Richard, in collaboration with Trude Krautheimer-Hess, *Lorenzo Ghiberti*, Princeton, Princeton University Press, 1970

Krautheimer, Richard, Spencer Corbett, Alfred K. Frazer, *Corpus Basilicarum Christianarum Romae*, Città del Vaticano, Pontificio Istituto di Archeologia Cristiana 1937-1977

Kugler, Hartmut, Sonja Glauch, Antje Wittig, *Die Elbstorfer W*eltkarte, Berlin, Akademie Verlag, 2007

Kynan-Wilson, William, "Subverting the Message: Master Gregory's Reception of and Response to the *Mirabilia Urbis Romae*", *Journal of Medieval History*, 44/3 (2018), pp. 347-364

Lanciani, Rodolfo, "Delle scoperte avvenute nei disteri pel Palazzo della Banca Nazionale", *Bullettino della Commissione Archeologica Comunale di Roma*, 14 (1886), pp. 184-191

Lanciani, Rodolfo, *Storia degli scavi di Roma*, Rome, E. Loescher, 1902

La Vere, Suzanne, "'A Priest is Not a Free Person': Clerical Sins and Upholding Higher Moral Standards in the *Gemma Ecclesiastica*", in *Gerald of Wales: New Perspectives on a Medieval Writer and Critic*, ed. by Georgia Henley and Joseph Mullen, Cardiff, University of Wales Press, 2018, pp. 183-202

Lembke, Katja, *Der Iseum Campense in Rom: Studie über den Isiskult unter Domitian*, Heidelberg, Verlag Archäologie und Geschichte, 1994

Lemmens, Leonhard, "De sancto Francisco Christum praedicante coram sultan Aegypti", *Archivum Franciscanum Historicum*, 19 (1926), pp. 559-578

Lloyd, Thomas, Julian Orbach, Robert Scourfield, *Pembrokeshire (The Buildings of Wales)*, New Haven, Yale University Press, 2004

Locke, Amy, *The Abbey of Evesham: The Victoria County History of the County of Worcester*, vol. II, ed. by John W. Willis-Bund, and William Page, London, Archibald Constable, 1906, pp. 112-119

Long, Jane L., "The Survival and Reception of the Classical Nude: Venus in the Middle Ages", in *The Meanings of Nudity in Medieval Art*, ed. by Sherry C. Lundquist, Burlington (VT), Ashgate, 2012, pp. 47-64

Luchterhand, Manfred, "Die Nacht der Bilder in Rom: die Kultgeschichte der päpstlichen Salvatorikone im Spiegel neuer Handschriften", in *Museum als Resonanzraum, Kunst Wissenschaft, Inszenierung Festschrift für Christoph Stiegemann*, ed. by Christiane Ruhmann and Petra Koch-Lüttke Westhues, Petersberg, Michael Imhof Verlag, 2020

Luchterhand, Manfred, "*Mirabilia* – Die Antiken Roms und ihre mittelalterlichen Betrachter", in *Wunder Roms im Blick des Nordens von der Antike bis zur Gegenwart*, ed. by Cristoph Stiegemann, Petersberg, Michael Imhof, 2017, pp. 90-109

Maccarrone, Michele, "*Ubi est papa, ibi est Roma*", in *Aus Kirche und Reich. Studien zu Theologie, Politik und Recht im Mittelalter. Festschrift für Friedrich Kempf zu seinem fünfundsiebzigsten Geburstag und fünfzigjährigen Doktorjubiläum*, ed. by Hubert Mordek, Sigmaringen, J. Thorbecke, 1983, pp. 371-382

Malmstrom, Ronald E., "The Twelfth Century Church of S. Maria in Capitolo and the Capitoline Obelisk", *Römisches Jahrbuch für Kunstgeschichte*, 16 (1976), pp. 1-16

Mansilla, Demetrio, "El Cardenal hispano Pelayo Gaitán (1206-1230)", *Anthologica Annua*, 1 (1953), pp. 11-66

Meecham-Jones, Simon, "Style, Truth and Irony: Listening to the Voice of Gerald of Wales's Writings", in *Gerald of Wales: New Perspectives on a Medieval Writer and Critic*, ed. by Georgia Henley and Joseph Mullen, Cardiff, University of Wales Press, 2018, pp. 127-144

Menzinger, Sara, "Viterbo, 'Città papale': motivazioni e conseguenze della presenza pontificia a Viterbo nel XIII secolo", in *Itineranza pontificia: mobilità della curia papale nel Lazio (secoli XII – XIII)*, ed. by Sandro Carocci, Rome, Istituto storico per il medioevo, 2003, pp. 307-340

Muñoz, Antonio, "La decorazione medioevale del Pantheon", *Nuovo Bullettino di Archeologia Cristiana*, 18 (1912), pp. 25-35

Neininger, Falko, *Konrad von Urach († 1227) Zähringer, Zisterzienser, Kardinal legat, (Quellen und Forschungen aus dem Gebiet der Geschichte NF 17)*, Paderborn, Schöningh, 1994

Nesselrath, Arnold, *Das Fossombroner Skizzenbuch*, London, The Warburg Institute, 1993

Nilgen, Ursula, "Amtsgenealogie und Amtsheiligkeit: Königs-und Bischofsreihe in der Kunstpropaganda des Hochmittelalters", in *Studien zur mittelalterlichen Kunst 800-1250. Festschrift für Florentine Mütherich zum 70. Geburtstag*, ed. by Katharina Bierbrauer, Peter Klein and Willibald Sauerländer, Munich, Prestel Verlag, 1985, pp. 217-234

Nilgen, Ursula, "Maria Regina – ein politischer Kultbildtypus", *Römisches Jahrbuch*, 19 (1981), pp. 3-33

Noehles, Karl, "Die Kunst der Cosmaten und die Idee der Renovatio Romae", in *Festschrift für Werner Hager*, ed. by Günter Fiensch and Max Imdahl, Recklinghausen, Bongers, 1966, pp. 17-27

O'Meara, John J., *Gerald of Wales: The History and Topography of Ireland*, London, Penguin Books, 1982

Oftestad, Eivor Andersen, *The Lateran Church in Rome and the Ark of the Covenant: Housing the Holy Relics of Jerusalem*, Cambridge, Cambridge University Press, 2019

Onians, John, *Bearers of Meaning: The Classical Orders in Antiquity, the Middle Ages and the Renaissance*, Princeton, Princeton University Press, 1988

Osborne, John, *Rome in the Eighth Century*, Cambridge, Cambridge University Press, 2020

Osborne, John, Amanda Claridge, *The Paper Museum of Cassiano del Pozzo, Series A, Antiquities and Architecture*, vol. II, *Early Christian and Medieval Antiquities, I Mosaics and Wall Paintings from Roman Churches*, London, Harvey Miller, 1996

Panofsky, Erwin, *Renaissance and Renascences in Western Art*, Stockholm, Almqvist & Wiksell, 1960

Papst und Kardinalskolleg von 1191 – bis 1214, ed. by Werner Maleczek, Vienna, Österreichischen Akademie der Wissenschaften, 1984 (Publikationen des Historischen Instituts beim Oesterreichischen Kulturinstitut in Rom, 1. Abt. Bd. 6)

Paravicini Bagliani, Agostino, *Cardinali di Curia e "familiae" cardinalizie dal 1227 – al 1254*, Padua, Antenore, 1972

Paravicini Bagliani, Agostino, *I testamenti dei cardinali del Duecento*, Rome, Società Romana di Storia Patria, 1980

Paravicini Bagliani, Agostino, *Il corpo del Papa*, Turin, Einaudi, 1994

Paravicini Bagliani, Agostino, "La mobilità della Curia Romana nel secolo XIII. Riflessi locali", in *Società e istituzioni dell'Italia comunale: l'esempio di Perugia (secoli XII – XIV), Perugia 6-9 novembre 1985*, Perugia, Deputazione di storia patria per l'Umbria, 1988, pp. 155-278 (updated version in *Itineranza pontificia*, pp. 3-78)

Payne, Mathew, Warwick Rodwell, "Edward the Confessor's Shrine in Westminster Abbey: Its Date of Construction Reconsidered", *Antiquaries Journal*, 97 (2017), pp. 187-204

Pelster, Franz, "Eine Kontroverse zwischen englischen Dominikanern und Minoriten über einige Punkte der Ordensregel", *Archivum Fratrum Praedicatorum*, 3 (1933), pp. 57-80

Petrus Capuanus Kardinal, Legat am vierten Kreuzzug, Theologe († 1214), ed. by Werner Maleczek, Vienna, Österreichischen Akademie der Wissenschaften, 1988 (Publikationen des Historischen Instituts beim Oesterreichischen Kulturinstitut in Rom, 1. Abt. Bd. 8)

Piron, Sylvain, "Avignon sous Jean XXII, l'Eldorado des théologiens", in *Jean XXII et le Midi* (*Cahiers de Fanjeaux 45*), ed. by Michelle Fournié and Daniel le Blévec, Toulouse, Privat, 2012, pp. 358-391

Powell, James M., *Anatomy of a Crusade*, Philadelphia, University of Pennsylvania Press, 1986

Powell, James M., "Honorius III's '*Sermo in Dedicatione Ecclesie Lateranensis*' and the Historical-Liturgical Traditions of the Lateran", *Archivum Historiae Pontificiae*, 21 (1983), pp. 195-209

Powicke, Maurice, "Gerald of Wales", *Bulletin of the John Rylands Library*, 12 (1928), pp. 389-410 (reprinted in Maurice Powicke, *The Christian Life in the Middle Ages*, Oxford, Oxford University Press, 1935, pp. 107-129)

Pulignani, Michele Faloci, *I marmorari romani a Sassovivo presso Foligno*, Perugia, Unione Tip. cooperativa, 1915

Pryce, Huw, "Gerald's Journey through Wales", *Journal of Welsh Ecclesiastical History*, 6 (1989), pp. 17-34

Quenstedt, Falk, Thilo Renz, "Kritik und Konstruktion der Wunderbaren in der Otia Imperialia des Gervasius von Tilbury", in *Das Wunderbaren Dimensionen einer Phänomene in Kunst und Kultur*, ed. by Stefanie Kreuzer and Uwe Durst, Paderborn, Wilhem Fink, 2018, pp. 251-262

Reh, Friedrich, *Kardinal Peter Capocci Ein Staatsmann und Feldherr des XIII. Jahrhunderts*, Berlin, Dr. Emil Ebering, 1933

Riccioni, Stefano, *Il mosaico absidale di S. Clemente a Roma. Exemplum della chiesa riformata*, Spoleto, Centro italiano di studi sull'alto medioevo, 2006

Richardson, Henry G., "Gervase of Tilbury", *History*, 46 (1961), pp. 102-114

Romano, Serena, *Il Duecento e la cultura gotica 1198-1287 ca*, Milan, Jaca Book, 2012

Romano, Serena, "L'icône *achieropiete* du Latran. Fonction d'une image absente", in *Art, Cérémonial et liturgie au Moyen Âge, Actes du colloque de 3e. Cycle Romand de Lettres, Lausanne-Fribourg, 24-25 mars, 14-15 avri, 12-13 mai, 2000*, ed. by Nicholas Bock, Peter Kurmann, Serena Romano and Jean-Michel Spieser, Rome, Viella, 2002, pp. 301-320

Romano, Serena, *Riforma e tradizione 1050-1198. La pittura medievale a Roma*, Milan, Jaca Book, 2006

Roosen-Runge, Heinz, "Ein Werke englischer Grossplastik des 13. Jahrhunderts and die Antike", in *Festschrift Hans R Hahnloser zum 60. Geburtstag 1959*, ed. by Ellen Beer and Paul Hofer, Basle, Birkhäuser, 1961, pp. 103-112

Roullet, Anne, *The Egyptian and Egyptianizing Monuments of Imperial Rome*, Leiden, Brill, 1972

Roullet, Anne H. M., *The Survival and Rediscovery of Egyptian Antiquities in Western Europe from Late Antiquity until the Close of the Sixteenth Century*, Ph.D. Dissertation, Oxford, 1969

Rubin, Jonathan, "Burchard of Mount Sion's *Descriptio Terrae Sanctae*: A Newly Discovered Extended Version", *Crusades*, 13 (2014), pp. 173-190

Russell, Ben, *The Economics of the Roman Stone Trade*, Oxford, Oxford University, 2013

Russell, Josiah C., *Dictionary of Writers of Thirteenth Century England*, London, Longmans Green, 1936

Salter, Herbert E., ed., *Snappe's Formulary and Other Records*, Oxford, Oxford University Press, 1924

Sauerländer, Willibald, "*Antiqui et Moderni* at Reims", *Gesta*, 42 (2003), pp. 19-37

Sayers, Jane, "English Benedictine Monks at the Papal Court in the Thirteenth Century: The Experience of Thomas of Marlborough in a Wider Context", *Journal of Medieval Monastic Studies*, 2 (2013), pp. 109-129

Sayers, Jane, "Robert of Somercotes", *Dictionary of National Biography*, vol. LI, p. 862

Schuster, Ildefonso. *La Basilica e il Monastero di S. Paolo fuori le Mura*, Turin, Società Editrice Internazionale, 1934

Schwarz, Michael Viktor, "Eine frühmittelalterliche Umgestaltung der Pantheon-Vorhalle", *Römisches Jahrbuch der Bibliotheca Hertziana*, 26 (1990), pp. 1-29

Schweitzer, Ursula, *Lőwe und Sphinx im alten Ägypten*, Glückstadt, J.J. Augustin, 1949

Scrinari, Valnea Santa Maria, *Il Laterano imperiale*, Città del Vaticano, Pontificio Istituto di Archeologia Cristiana, 1991-1997

Shearman, John, "Raphael, Rome and the Codex Escurialensis", *Master Drawings*, 15 (1977), pp. 107-146

Short, Ian, "Literary Culture at the Court of Henry II", in *Henry II: New Interpretations*, ed. by Christopher Harper-Bill and Nicholas Vincent, Woodbridge, Boydell and Brewer, 2007, pp. 335-361

Silanos, Pietro, "Niccolò Chiaramonti", *Dizionario Biografico degli Italiani*, vol. LXXVIII, Rome, Istituto della Enciclopedia italiana, 2013, pp. 385-387

Silanos, Pietro, "Ottone da Tonengo", *Dizionario Biografico degli Italiani*, vol. LXXX, Rome, Istituto della Enciclopedia italiana, 2014, pp. 4-7

Smith, Joshua B., *Walter Map and the Matter of Britain*, University Park, University of Pennsylvania Press, 2017

Smith, R.R.R., *Antinous Boy Made God*, Catalogue of an exhibition at the Ashmolean Museum, Oxford 28 September 2018 – 24 February 2019, Oxford, Ashmolean Museum, 2018

Spaethen, M., "Giraldus Cambrensis und Thomas von Evesham über die von ihnen an der Kurie geführten Prozesse", *Neues Archiv*, 31 (1906), pp. 595-649

Stewart, Andrew, "A Tale of Seven Nudes: The Capitoline and Medici Aphrodites, Four Nymphs at Elean Herakleia and Aphrodite at Megalopolis", *Antichthon*, 44 (2010), pp. 12-32

Stewart, Susan, *The Ruins: Lesson, Meaning, and Material in Western Culture*, Chicago, Chicago University Press, 2020

Stiegemann, Cristoph, ed., *Wunder Roms im Blick des Nordens von der Antike bis zur Gegenwart*, Petersberg, Michael Imhof, 2017

Stones, Alison, "Le culte de Saint Jacques entre Compostelle et Pistoia et le rôle du chanoine Rainerius", in *Pèlerinages, origines, succès et avenir*, ed. by Térence Le Deschaut de Manredon, Cahors, Éditions patrimoniales de la ville de Cahors, 2019, pp. 39-48

Strzelczyk, Jerzy, *Gerwasy z Tilbury Studium z dziejów uczoności geograficznej w średniowieczu*, Warsaw, Zakład Narodowy im Ossolińskich, 1970

Tatton-Brown, Tim, "The Two Great Marble Pavements in the Sanctuary and Shrine Areas of Canterbury Cathedral and Westminster Abbey", in *Historic Floors: Their Care and Conservation*, ed. by Jane Fawcett, Oxford, Butterworth-Heinemann, 2007, pp. 53-62

Taylor, John, *The "Universal Chronicle" of Ranulph Higden*, Oxford, Oxford University Press, 1966

Tellenbach, Gerd, "Zur Frühgeschichte abendländischer Reisebeschreibungen", in *Historia Integra Festschrift für Erich Hassinger zum 70. Geburtstag*, ed. by Hans Fenske, Wolfgang Reinhard and Ernst Schulin, Berlin, Duncker und Humblot, 1977, pp. 51-80

The Basilica of Saint John Lateran to 1600, ed. by Lex Bosman, Ian Haynes and Paolo Liverani, Cambridge, Cambridge University Press, 2020

Thompson Lee, Anne, "The Ruin: Bath or Babylon? A Non-Archaeological Investigation", *Neuphilologische Mitteilungen*, 74 (1973), pp. 443-455

Thorpe, Lewis, "Walter Map and Gerald of Wales", *Medium Aevum*, 47/1 (1978), pp. 6-21

Thunø, Erik, "The Pantheon in the Middle Ages", in *The Pantheon from Antiquity to the Present*, ed. by Tod Marder and Mark Wilson Jones, Cambridge, Cambridge University Press, 2015, pp. 231-252

Tillmann, Helene, *Papst Innocenz III*, Bonn, Röhrscheid, 1954

Tolan, John, *Saint Francis and the Sultan: The Curious History of a Christian-Muslim Encounter*, Oxford, Oxford University Press, 2009

Tomei, Alessandro, *Iacobus Torriti Pictor*, Rome, Argos, 1990

Tomlin, Roger S. O., Richard G. Annis, "A Roman Altar from Carlisle Castle", *Transactions of the Cumberland and Westmorland Antiquarian and Archaeological Society*, 89 (1989), pp. 77-92

Twyman, Susan, *Papal Ceremonial at Rome in the Twelfth Century*, Martlesham, Boydell Press, 2010

Vale, Malcolm, *The Princely Court: Medieval Courts and Culture in North-West Europe*, Oxford, Oxford University Press, 2001

Vitali, Samuele, "'*Sicut exploratoret spoliorum cupidus*'. Zu Methode und Funktion der Antiken-rezeption bei Nikolaus von Verdun", *Wiener Jahrbuch für Kunstgeschichte*, 52 (2002), pp. 9-46

Vöge, Wilhelm, "Bahnbrecher des Naturstudiums um 1200", *Zeitschrift für bildende Kunst*, 24 (1914), pp. 193-216 (reprinted in *Bildhauer des Mittelalters. Gesammelte Studien von Wilhelm Vöge*, Berlin, Gebr. Mann, 1958, pp. 63-97)

von den Brincken, Anna-Dorothee, "Islam und Oriens Christianus in den Schriften des Domscholasters Oliver († 1227)", in *Orientalische Kultur und Europäisches Mittelalter*, ed. by Albert Zimmermann, Ingrid Craemer-Ruegenberg and Gudrun Vuillemin-Diem, Berlin, De Gruyter, 1985, pp. 86-102

Walker, Ronald F., *Medieval Pembrokeshire*, vol. II, Haverfordwest, Pembrokeshire Historical Society, 2002

Walter, Christopher, "Papal Political Imagery in the Medieval Lateran Palace", *Cahiers Archéologiques*, 20 (1970), pp. 155-176

Walter, Christopher, "Papal Political Imagery in the Medieval Lateran Palace, part 2", *Cahiers Archéologiques*, 21 (1971), pp. 109-136

Walton, Michael, "Actors, Chorus and Masks", in *The Art of Ancient Greek Theater*, ed. by Mary L. Hart, Los Angeles, J. Paul Getty Museum, 2010, pp. 33-41

Ward-Perkins, John, "Roman Architecture" in *Etruscan and Roman Architecture*, ed. by Axel Boëthius and John Ward Perkins, Harmondsworth, Penguin Books, 1970

Weber, Heinrich, *Über das Verhältniss Englands zu Rom während der Zeit der Legation des Cardinal Othos in den Jahren 1237-1241*, Berlin, Weidmannsche Buchhandlung, 1883

Westminster Abbey: The Cosmati Pavements, ed. by Lindy Grant and Richard Mortimer, Aldershot, Ashgate, 2002

Wickham, Chris, *Medieval Rome*, Oxford, Oxford University Press, 2015

Wiek, Peter, "Das Strassburger Münster Untersuchungen über die Mitwirkung des Stadtbürgertums am Bau bischöflicher Kathedralkirchen im Spätmittelalter", *Zeitschrift für die Geschichte des Oberrheins*, 107 (1959), pp. 40-113

Willemsen, Carl, *Kaiser Friedrichs II. Triumphtor zu Capua*, Wiesbaden, Insel Verlag, 1953

Williamson, Dorothy, "Some Aspects of the Legation of Cardinal Otto in England, 1237-1241", *English Historical Review*, 64 (1949), pp. 145-173

Williamson, Paul, *Gothic Sculpture 1140-1300*, London/New Haven, Yale University Press, 1995

Wilpert, Josef, "L'Acheropita, ossia l'immagine del Salvatore nella Cappella del Sancta Sanctorum", *L'Arte*, 10 (1907), pp. 161-177

Winckelmann, Johan, *Sammtliche Werke, Geschichte de Kunst*, 8, ed. by Joachim Eiselein, Donauöschingen, O. Zeller, 1825-1835

Wittkower, Rudolph, "Hieroglyphics in the Early Renaissance", in *Developments in the Early Renaissance. Papers of the Second Annual Conference of the Center for Medieval and Early Renaissance Studies, State University of New York at Binghampton, 4-5 May 1968*, ed. by Bernard S. Levy, Albany, Center for Medieval and Early Renaissance Studies, 1968, pp. 58-97

Wolf, Armin, "Ikonologie der Ebstorfer Weltkarte und politische Situation des Jahres 1239 Zum Weltbild des Gervasius von Tilbury am welfischen Hofe", in *Ein Weltbild vor Columbus. Die Ebstorfer Weltkarte. Interdiziplinäres Kolloquium*, ed. by Hartmut Kugler and Eckhard Michael, Weinheim, VCH Acta Humaniora, 1988, pp. 54-119

Wolf, Gerhard, *Salus Populi Romani Die Geschichte römischer Kultbilder im Mittelalter*, Weinheim, VCH Acta Humaniora, 1990

Wolff, Étienne, "Un voyageur à Rome au XII – XIII siècle: Magister Gregorius", *Bulletin de l'Association Guillaume Budé*, 1 (2005), pp. 163-171

Wollesen, Jens, *Die Fresken von San Piero a Grado bei Pisa*, Bad, Oeynhausen, 1977

Worstbrock, Franz Josef, "Review of Nine Robintje Miedema, *Die 'Mirabilia Romae'. Untersuchungen ihre Überlieferung mit Edition der deutschen und niederländischen Texte (Münchener Texte und Untersuchungen zur deutschen Literatur des Mittelalters, Bd.108*), Tübingen, Niemeyer, 1996", *Zeitschrift für deutches Altertum und deutsches Literatur*, 126/1 (1997), pp. 116-130

Yapp, Brunsdon, *Birds in Medieval Manuscripts*, London, The British Library, 1981

Zandri, Giuliana, "No. 15 Reliquario, Ponzano Romano from S.Andrea in Flumine", *Tesori d'Arte Sacra di Roma e del Lazio dal Medioevo all'Ottocento, Palazzo delle Esposizione* Novembre – Dicembre, Rome, Assessorato Antichità, Belle Arti e Problemi della Cultura, 1975, pp. 11-12

Zutshi, Patrick, "Innocent III and the Reform of the Papal Chancery", in *Innocenzo III Urbis et Orbis. Atti del Congresso internazionale (Roma, 9-15 settembre 1998*), vol. I, ed. by Andrea Sommerlechner, Rome, Istituto storico italiano per il medioevo, 2003, pp. 84-101

Index of Names

Finito di stampare
nel mese di settembre 2022
da The Factory s.r.l.
Roma